Open access edition supported by the National Endowment for the Humanities /
Andrew W. Mellon Foundation Humanities Open Book Program.

© 2019 Johns Hopkins University Press
Published 2019

Johns Hopkins University Press
2715 North Charles Street
Baltimore, Maryland 21218-4363
www.press.jhu.edu

ISBN-13: 978-1-4214-3455-1 (open access)
ISBN-10: 1-4214-3455-5 (open access)

ISBN-13: 978-1-4214-3453-7 (pbk. : alk. paper)
ISBN-10: 1-4214-3453-9 (pbk. : alk. paper)

ISBN-13: 978-1-4214-3454-4 (electronic)
ISBN-10: 1-4214-3454-7 (electronic)

This page supersedes the copyright page included in the original publication of this work.

T0366965

SCIENCE AT THE WHITE HOUSE

Edward J. Burger, Jr., M.D.

SCIENCE AT THE WHITE HOUSE

A POLITICAL

LIABILITY

THE JOHNS HOPKINS UNIVERSITY PRESS: BALTIMORE AND LONDON

The Johns Hopkins University Press, Baltimore, Maryland 21218
The Johns Hopkins Press Ltd., London

Library of Congress Cataloging in Publication Data

Burger, Edward J
    Science at the White House.

    Includes bibliographical references and index.
    1. Science and state–United States. 2. Presidents–United
States. I. Title. [DNLM: 1. Government–United States.
2. Science–United States. 3. Health policy–United States.
Q127.U6 B899s]
Q127.U6B83   338.973   80-81425
ISBN 0-8018-2433-8

To SGB, whose advice I have always highly valued

It is always a little silly to give advice, but to give good advice
is absolutely fatal.
—Oscar Wilde, *Portrait of Mr. W. H.*

Science is a first-rate piece of furniture for a man's upper chamber,
if he has common sense on the ground floor.
—Oliver Wendell Holmes, *The Poet at the Breakfast Table*

CONTENTS

Figures

FOREWORD

After the atomic bomb gave an aura of omniscience to scientists, and after the manned landings on the moon led some politicians to assume that technology could accomplish nearly any purpose in their parties' platforms, students of government developed a keen interest in the role of the President's scientific advisers.

Americans had come rather late to a serious consideration of the role of science in public affairs. Revolutionary ideology gave science a leading role in European political theory and made it seem the key to political issues. There were indeed perceptive Americans in earlier generations, from Thomas Jefferson and Benjamin Franklin on to the National Resources Planning Board of the New Deal era, who were concerned with the use of science for public ends. But the dominant leadership of the scientific societies, especially in the physical sciences with their ties through engineering to industry, remained on principle aloof from politics and preferred to have no financial support from tax funds.

When World War II converted the scientific community to a new view of their relation to government, the physical scientists, who had played the decisive role in weapons development, were its dominant leaders for a generation. Many of them, and many of their allies in the applied social sciences—operations researchers and systems analysts—came first to have grandiose ideas about the extent to which scientific advisers could answer the big questions of public policy, and then, sometimes in disillusionment with government over such issues as the Viet Nam war or environmental pollution, came to despair of any benefits from participation in the governmental establishment.

It may now be possible to develop a more discriminating perspective, as the main public issues in which science is involved are no longer primarily in the military, atomic, or space programs. In basic research, more Federal money is now spent on health and medical sciences than on any other category. Whether or not the Supreme Court, as Mr. Dooley remarked, follows the election returns, the science advisers to the President must follow the fluctuations in federal grants and contracts.

Dr. Burger's book, therefore, comes at an opportune time. The original, rather inflated hopes of some of the early observers of the President's science advisers—the observers tended to have more grandiose ideas than the advisers themselves—have been scaled down as the result of President Nixon's estrangement from his scientific critics, and his abolition of the President's Science Advisory Committee. Now a new range of issues, many of them in the fields of medicine and health, occupy the news headlines and challenge politicians and bureaucrats. Genetic manipulation, abortion, the pollution of the environment, population control, health and hospital insurance—these issues raise a different type of question for scientists to worry about. They are not issues in which the government, as the exclusive buyer (as it is in the military or space programs), can readily control decisions or be granted by the electorate an authoritative voice because of the demands of national defense. They are issues in which the average citizen and the average family feel a keen personal interest, an interest in which considerations of economics and even health are sometimes overridden by intense moral convictions.

By concentrating on his experience with such issues as national health policy, biomedical research and development, regulation of environmental pollution, and population and family planning, Dr. Burger is able to raise significant questions with respect to the role of scientific advice in the American political system. Without the protection of the veil of secrecy that is still tolerated in military and national security affairs, the questions regarding the analysis of policy and of the means of its execution are no more shielded from political scrutiny—as long as Congressional committees and the press continue their present habits—than is the final decision on the ends and values of policy.

Indeed, Dr. Burger asks whether the very sophistication of our present analytic methods does not make the job of policy decision more difficult for the chief executive. Can science make its contribution to government programs best by helping decide the fundamental issues, or can it be permitted in a democratic system to make its contribution only after the basic value choices have been made? Dr. Burger poses these questions for us in a challenging way.

The reader may well go on to ask whether these are aspects of the business of scientific advice that distinguish it from other forms of expert staff work—the contributions of the lawyer, the economist, or the administrative analyst—or whether scientists are now simply being subjected to constraints that older hands in the business of politics have had to tolerate for many years. Or perhaps there is something deeper in the problem: perhaps scientists, realizing that they do not keep their skills up to date by administrative staff work, feel compelled to cultivate close ties with colleagues in research institutions in ways that make it especially difficult for them to maintain the institutional discipline and the confidentiality that are essential for policy staff work at the highest political level.

Dr. Burger is inclined to think that, on balance, scientific advice has become a political liability in the White House. This was, of course, President Nixon's conclusion, which led him to abolish the President's Science Advisory Committee. I come to the opposite conclusion, believing that it is indispensable in the contemporary world, and that alternative ways, including some that he suggests, must be developed to provide it for the President.

No one is likely to have the last word on such issues for a considerable time to come, but Dr. Burger has provided us not only with much of the basic information that can serve as the foundation for critical analysis but also with some challenging interpretations of his own, which all students of American government, and especially of the relation of the sciences to public policy, will do well to ponder.

Don K. Price

PREFACE

This book grew out of my experience in the early 1970s in the Office of Science and Technology, the supporting staff for the science adviser to the President. As a physician and a scientist, I had come to that position after several years on the faculty at Harvard, where I had been engaged in biomedical research and teaching. Fortunately, my preparation for Washington had been broadened through a joint appointment at the John F. Kennedy School of Government, whicy gave me an initial window on the world of science policy.

I had been warned by my predecessors more than once before coming to Washington that one of the things one did *not* do as a member of the presidential science advisory apparatus was to sit back and make something called science policy. The instructions about what one *was* supposed to do, however, were less clear.

My initiation ceremony was as abrupt as it was instructive. As I walked through the halls of government for the first time, I was handed the issue of 2, 4, 5-T—the shorthand chemical designation for a herbicide used heavily in the United States and as a defoliant in the war in Southeast Asia. 2, 4, 5-T was implicated as a cause of birth defects among those born of mothers exposed to the chemical. 2, 4, 5-T exploded suddenly as a political/scientific issue with a large number of derivative and far-reaching aspects. This one issue became immediately instructive in indicating the dimensions of the subjects which were to link the public policy machinery to the world of science.

There followed for me a long series of issues covering a very wide territory. The menu of activities brought to the science adviser's office is inevitably a broad one. In my case, it covered such items as nutrition and the world food question, national health insurance, medical education and policies for the training of physicians, family planning and population, regulation designed to protect human health and the integrity of the physical environment, and policies governing the federal support of biomedical research.

There were a great many short-term issues—protection of uranium miners from exposure to ionizing radiation, bilateral international scientific exchanges with a variety of nations, the establishment of air pollution standards, appointment of the directors of the National Institutes of Health and the National Cancer Program, and interaction with a constant stream of legislative initiatives. An anchoring feature with recurrent and periodic aspects was the budget process of the executive branch. The annual budget "cycle" reached a climax each fall (budget season) in a ritual of supplication, special pleading, and final decision. Somewhat in the spirit of a newspaper reporter, each member of the staff of the Office of Science and Technology had his own "beat" or territory made up of the agencies which corresponded to his professional skills and interests.

There was, however, an array of longer-term issues. Here the process of articulation with the public policy machinery became substantially less effective. The reasons for this became apparent. In part, they turned around matters of timing. The democratic political process is by nature a responsive one. Public policy issues raised well ahead of time are of academic importance to public office holders whose terms are only two or four years. At the other extreme, issues which are so imminent that no deliberate decision making can be influential are outside the realm of useful manipulation by politicians. Consideration of these is similarly academic. The window of opportunity was a narrow one and it focused principally on issues just over the horizon—likely to break on the public scene within the foreseeable future.

However, there were more fundamental problems that colored the match between the science adviser and his advisee. One of these problem areas was an inevitable dual role for the science adviser. This concerned the duality of functions of supposed advocate or at least representative of the interests of the scientific community on the one hand and objective, third-party counsel on important national issues on the other. The Science Adviser did have a constituency of sorts of his own—generally in the academic scientific community. However, compared to his counterpart, the chairman of the Council on Environmental Quality, the science adviser's following was always less well organized, less vocal, and less of a political force.* This conflict between

---

*The dual role played by the Council on Environmental Quality has generally proved to be an impossible one. In part because the chairman of the CEQ represented a large vocal constituency of environmentalists, the effectiveness of the CEQ in dealing with "inside" matters, national projects and issues, was substantially diminished over time.

"inside" and "outside" interests was probably not as prominent as some observers of the scene have contended.

There were, in a sense, far larger problems. These turned around fundamental differences between the incentives that were important to politicians and those that operated on scientists and engineers who staffed the Office of Science and Technology. This fundamental conflict was nowhere more apparent than in those instances where the Science Adviser attempted to embrace a fundamental issue with far-reaching implications for the nation. If a President really wished to improve the health of the American populace, where should his initiatives be directed to be most effective? What was regulation, designed nominally to protect against hazards of environmental chemicals or unsafe medical devices or ionizing radiation, really "purchasing" in the way of health? What was the value of national investments in fundamental biological and medical research toward the improvement in health of the population? Questions such as these, which at least one line of logic could judge to be fundamental to reasonable policy making, were of little use to the public policy machinery in real life. Worse than that, there was frequently an active fear generated whenever study was begun for such a question. To address such broad questions deliberately and analytically was to question conventional wisdom on several fronts and threatened (if only on paper) to disrupt elements of national stability. Such an activity too closely borders on the stuff of national planning—an activity not known for its political attractiveness in the United States.

The present book reflects a period of experience. It seeks to compare the nominal charter for the President's science adviser and his staff with the realities of that office. It is a view of that White House function over a brief period of six years. During those years, I volunteered some ideas to others in the form of published papers and talks before professional peers. I was urged to share some of these ideas with a broader audience. Two of the published papers have been drawn upon rather heavily for a portion of this present book, although the original material was adapted and brought up to date. In this regard, I am indebted to the Elsevier Publishing Company for permission to reprint and otherwise reflect portions of an article published in 1976 in *Technological Forecasting and Social Change* (in Chapter 2) and to the Federation of American Societies for Experimental Biology for material first seen in *Federation Proceedings* in 1975 (in Chapter 4).

I am immensely grateful to a number of my colleagues who brought their own experience and wisdom to bear in critical reading and commentary of the early drafts of the manuscript. In this regard I am pleased to acknowledge the very constructive assistance of Louis Hellman, William D. Carey, Gabor

Strasser, and Daniel Margolies. Finally and importantly, I am highly in-debted to Kathleen Jerome, whose always careful editorial assistance and preparation of the manuscript were essential ingredients in bringing it into the world.

SCIENCE AT THE WHITE HOUSE

1. INTRODUCTION

The Office of the Science Adviser to the President had its origins in an era of a large, national project—World War II. It was "born again" and put into its present institutional form during the time of another national project— the national space program.

The true origins, in fact, run much deeper. They include a much longer history of an evolving relationship between science, scientists, and the federal government. As historians of science have often pointed out, the scientific sectors that early received government encouragement and assistance would clearly be thought of today as "applied" science. Science as it contributed to government was, by design, related to matters of commerce and industry and to the opening of the new nation. Surveying of land was of obvious importance. Charting of coastal waters by the Coast and Geodetic Survey was one of the first engagements of the government with science. Mapping of the interior of the new nation—a companion to exploration—was another. Science for a productive agricultural industry was a third primary governmental preoccupation with science. Here, in particular, the government effort was sizable, prolonged, and highly successful. The story of the establishment of the land grant colleges, of the Agricultural Extension Service, and of the numerous other facets of the government's fostering of science for agriculture and of education of the agricultural community about the results of scientific investigation, is a rich and well-documented saga.[1]

However, perhaps not unexpectedly, it was the demands of war in particular that mobilized scientific talent in behalf of government service. The National Academy of Sciences was chartered by Congress and formed in 1863 expressly to bring advice and guidance on scientific and technical matters to the government in time of civil war. As World War I approached, the National

Academy of Sciences stepped forward to put itself in the service of the government. Further, the National Research Council of the academy was organized expressly to assist in behalf of national defense.[2]

The evolution of the presidential science advisory function, however, was not simply a reflection of increasing government involvement in scientific research and development. It was much more a result of an ever-increasing complexity and technical character of national programs and national endeavors in which the federal establishment had great interest. Government involvement has come about through sponsorship, performance, creation of incentive, or regulation. Because of the increasing technical complexity of programs and projects (and consequently, of the public policy issues surrounding them) it was reasoned that expert technical and scientific judgment and orderly and timely access to expert scientific advice in the Office of the President would enhance and inform the deliberations and judgments that the government made. At the same time, incumbents in the White House hoped such mechanisms would enhance their own capacity in the context of political bargaining.

Thus, for several decades there has been a liaison of sorts between science and scientists on the one hand and the public policy machinery of the Office of the President on the other. During this short history, that liaison has undergone a number of metamorphoses. The liaison had been alternatively strengthened and weakened (almost entirely on the basis of the desires of the incumbent President). Individual presidential judgment concerning whether and how to use his science adviser rested typically on matters such as the degree to which the nation was willing to allow its government to arrogate powers to itself in the national interest. (The electorate has given its President a clearer consensus for action and initiative in times of the national distresses of war and depression.) Secondly, science and scientists were more actively sought out by the White House when it was clear to the electorate that major issues facing the country were marked by a high technical content. The manned space program and the program for exploration of resources beneath the sea are examples. Finally, perhaps, an overlying factor in determining to what extent the public policy machinery looks to scientists for advice is the view at the time by the public of science and of derivatives of science. During those times when a nation warmly embraces science and technology and sees them as desirable partners in the enhancement of the economy or the advancement of the physical frontiers, a President finds it to his advantage to take active steps to look to the scientific community for help in formulating national decisions. A popular view of science and technology as antithetical to national well-being, however, discourages any manifestly close relationship between the White House and science.

There has been a further factor that has colored the form and the closeness of the ties between the scientific community and the Office of the President. This is the view held by scientists of the government. For most of the nation's history, science had meant academic science. University-based scientists traditionally sought to guard an independence from government influence and control over the conduct of research. Related to this was a fear that involvement in the political process carried with it a hazard of influence by the state —an evil to be avoided at almost any cost. This view has been tempered in recent years when scientists agreed to accept large amounts of public monies for the support of research.

President Franklin D. Roosevelt appointed a Board of Scientific Advisers in 1933. The arguments used by the proponents of this arrangement were the assistance which such a board could give to the formulation of agricultural programs and to the modernization of the Weather Bureau. The scientific establishment was clearly ambivalent about this new role. The National Academy of Sciences, upstaged by the appointment of a new board, sought in vain to frustrate the board's creation. The board did provide some useful but narrowly divided counsel on matters of scientific content of certain government programs. However, according to one chronicler, the members of the Science Advisory Board evinced "indifference toward the political environment" in which they operated.[3]

Consideration of political *realities* was alien to most Science Advisory Board members, who wanted politicians to appreciate the needs of science but who had little interest in the desires or needs of politicians.[4]

Within two years of its formation, the Science Advisory Board was permitted to expire. Roosevelt's National Resources Planning Board sought limited scientific assistance (from the National Academy of Sciences). However, this role was not to be a continuous one.

The National Resources Planning Board looked briefly to the academy for advice on how science might contribute to national planning. However, as Don Price correctly reminds us, "the political gulf between FDR and the conservative leaders of the scientific community was much too wide, even before Congress decided to put an end to such nonsense as planning by abolishing the board."[5]

The thesis of this book is that the liaison between science (and scientists) and the public policy machinery at the corporate level of the government is a difficult and tenuous one at best—in any era. David Beckler, long the executive secretary of the President's Science Advisory Committee, observed that forces of rejection have operated to limit the influence of the White House science advisory mechanism—beginning as early as the time of its establishment.[6] In this fundamental observation Beckler is correct. The reasons are to be found in certain intrinsic differences between how scientists think about national matters and the incentives which operate so strongly on politicians.

There is no need to invoke a conspiratorial theory to explain this point. There are simply important differences between the outlooks of those who assume political leadership and those who are trained in and dedicated to the rigors of science. The description of the fits and starts between scientists and government in Roosevelt's time point to the fact that the potential for rejection—the gulf between the two sides—is not a new phenomenon. As will be seen later, neither is it confined to the Executive Office or the White House. In my view, however, the differences separating scientists and government have become sharper in recent years—principally because of changes in the pattern of government in recent years as a by-product of public demands for greater accountability.

It has been traditional and convenient to divide the functions of the presidential science advisory apparatus into two categories. One of these, sometimes described as policy making for science, concerns judgments about how much government money should be spent in support of research and development and how these monies should be allocated among various categories of research and development. This is the role of perhaps most interest to scientists and professionals who understand that the well-being of science and its institutions is a direct function of the federal willingness to support research and development. The other function, which others have termed science for policy making, is a quite different matter. Science for policy making is the application of scientific and technical information, of scientists' judgments and, perhaps, of some of the methods of science to decisions about governmental programs and policies—especially for those programs and policies that have clear scientific and technical components.

From the point of view of the nation and the government, this second category, science for policy making, is clearly the more important of the two functions. It is here that the science advisory function has the potential for making the greatest contribution to large and important decisions and to policy choices affecting large amounts of money, rearrangements of national life and the well-being of large numbers of people. My judgment is that, while this function is of undeniable importance, its execution in practice—particularly for nonmilitary and nonsecurity issues—is rendered difficult by the very processes of democratic government as we know them. In fact, the better the job done by a science adviser, the more skill that is used in his analysis and advice, the more hazardous is the process for the adviser. The adviser who proceeds as a scientifically oriented man (or even a logical man) is by definition likely to find himself in waters dangerously close to the processes known as governmental planning—a concept that is not well received by the electorate.

Policy making and priority setting in general imply analysis and planning. On the one hand, the case is compelling for a mechanism or mechanisms to engage broad and systematic analysis for decision making and priority setting. Yet the agonizing paradox is the strong injunction to any serious effort within the governmental structure—at least for nonmilitary aspects of national life.

Those trained in the rigors of scientific investigation—in the search for scientific "truths" and the understanding of natural phenomena—are steeped in the practices and philosophy of objective and analytic thinking. What scientists can bring to the office of a presidential counsellor is analytic thinking, careful sorting of alternatives, quantitative comparisons, and evaluation combined with an eye toward future trends. It is these very aspects, in fact, that nominally have been included in the charters granted to the Office of the Science Adviser.[7] Yet, as logical as this matter appears on the surface, in practice, to the extent that these activities resemble planning in areas such as health, energy, education, housing, or transportation, they are not necessarily well received by an electorate whose own interests may be threatened. Explicit analysis and planning for domestic issues cut across the grain of traditional consensus building and may at times be looked upon as actually interfering with the public policy process.

The chapters that follow are an attempt to examine this paradoxical proposition that science advice for the President—particularly that portion of it identified as science for policy making—fits uncomfortably with the public policy machinery. The first of the following chapters attempts to lay a historical perspective. The general proposition is seen not to be a new phenomenon, nor is it restricted to the White House. However, the marriage is perhaps an even more difficult one now than it was in earlier times—in spite of the best and most rational will to make it work. Chapters 3, 4, 5, and 6 (the bulk of the book) represent the text for the sermon. These chapters deal with specific substantive issues—areas of domestic programs and policy making with which the author had personal involvement and experience as a member of the Office of the President's Science Adviser between 1969 and 1976.

2. SCIENCE ADVICE FOR THE PRESIDENT:
A PERSPECTIVE

Evolution of the Presidential Advisory Mechanism

Vannevar Bush, perhaps, deserves the title of the first real presidential science adviser. There had been earlier attempts—particularly during the presidency of F. D. Roosevelt—to bring the benefits of science and the judgments of scientists into the White House. The appointment of Bush, however, as head of the Office of Scientific Research and Development, was the first serious attempt to couple scientific talent to the public policy machinery. Vannevar Bush's fundamental charter was to mobilize science and its offspring, technology, in behalf of pursuing a successful conclusion to a World War. In this, he and his institution, the OSRD, were eminently successful. Bush later described himself as the "scientific adviser" to the President on "civilian scientific matters."[1] In performing this role, Bush saw himself as a link between the White House and the scientific and engineering communities.

The faith that was born of that now famous wartime experience was that the potential of science to help realize the betterment of human welfare, broadly speaking, was enormous but had barely been realized. The wartime record was held up as the model to be followed broadly. Optimism in general, and for the potential of science in particular, was at a high level. Roosevelt's letter to Bush at the end of the war, inviting the latter's appraisal of how best to utilize science for society's needs generally, proposed that the government had only begun to utilize science in the nation's welfare.[2]

A key question concerned the proper form of the coupling. The admitted success of the OSRD experience was great. The national goal of winning a war was of extreme importance. This goal was not subject to national debate.

Rather, the war mobilized the electorate and "made it possible to cut against the grain of our political habits and prejudices."[3] The particular institutional form of the OSRD was important. In Vannevar Bush's own appraisal, the two elements of greatest importance in regard to form were direct reporting to the President and funds of its own.[4] A third element of importance was the fact that its work was transacted in secret—entirely out of the public's view. This again removed its activities from the give and take of political debate. Finally, there is every indication that the President *desired* the counsel of his scientific adviser.

Science, the Endless Frontier, Vannevar Bush's report to the President, urged that it was in the national interest to foster the growth and prosperity of science through public support.[5] That notion was certainly accepted. Beginning in 1946, the Atomic Energy Commission was created, the Office of Naval Research was established, and the activities of the National Institutes of Health were placed into a mode of expansion which would not even begin to slow until the mid-1960s. However, the National Research Foundation, called for in Bush's report, eluded creation for half a decade. Its ultimate realization, in the form of the National Science Foundation, was due in part to expressed concerns over a "lack of coordination" among the evolving breadth of governmental scientific investments and, once again, to a new war —this time in Korea. In 1947, President Truman received five volumes of a report on federal scientific research (the "Steelman Report").[6] This, in effect, complemented the Vannevar Bush report of two years before. It recommended, among other things, a member of the White House staff for scientific liaison and an Interdepartmental Committee for Scientific Research.[7] In 1951, President Truman attached eleven of the nation's top scientists to a Science Advisory Committee of the Office of Defense Mobilization. This body, the first of its kind to be implanted in the Executive Office of the President, was to "advise the President and the Mobilization Director on matters relating to scientific research and development for defense."[8]

In 1957, the Science Advisory Committee became the *President's* Science Advisory Committee. President Eisenhower became persuaded of his need for objective and technically sound advice—especially on matters of military and security issues. He responded positively to the urging of one of his own counsellors and appointed a special assistant to the President for science and technology. The first to hold that position was James Killian, an engineer, president of MIT, and a member of the President's Science Advisory Committee (PSAC). Again (and importantly), this new and evolving entity was looked to principally for advice on military matters and on issues of national security.

Most of the elements of what were to become the "science advisory mechanism" were now in place. The special assistant to the President was effectively the science adviser. The President's Science Advisory Committee was a visible and well-regarded vehicle for gathering expert advice from the scientific establishment in behalf of governmental and national decisions. A third element was put in place two years later in 1959 with the establishment of the Federal Council on Science and Technology. The Federal Council, composed of the highest ranking members of each federal agency responsible for science and technology, was designed to bring about an element of "coordination" of federal science and research.

Dr. George Kistiakowsky, who succeeded Killian in 1959 as special assistant for science and technology, continued in the pattern of his predecessor. As in Killian's case, Kistiakowsky's principal concerns were in fields of military and national security issues. His diary of those years reveals, for example, a sizable fraction of his effort and time devoted to technical aspects of a nuclear test ban treaty.*[9] A new (but similar) preoccupation for the science adviser, the national space program, became prominent after the Russians orbited Sputnik I in 1957. In a sense, this set of issues was simply an extension of the general area of science and technology for military and national security purposes. At the same time, however, the electorate became fascinated by the combination of advances in both science and national prestige that were thought possible through a civilian space program. This latter eventually galvanized the electorate in behalf of a program of manned lunar exploration.

In the early 1960s, important changes occurred in the pattern of presidential science advice. Dr. Jerome Wiesner replaced Kistiakowsky as special assistant in March 1961. A subcommittee of the Senate Government Operations Committee was moving toward recommendations for organizational changes in the President's office to improve the application of science and technology in behalf of defense and security. These recommendations culminated in a proposal for a specific organizational structure, a much augmented staff, a series of specific and structured activities, and a statutory basis for those activities.[10] Partly as a result of these pressures from the legislature, the President transmitted to the Congress on March 29, 1962, a Reorganization Plan that formally established the Office of Science and Technology and brought together the functions of the President's science adviser.[11] A part of the process of "institutionalizing" the science advisory apparatus was to place in the hands of the President's science adviser some of the functions that had

---

*An exception occurred when Kistiakowsky became embroiled in the controversy over the use of a herbicide, aminotriazole, in the growing of cranberries.

been in the charter of the National Science Foundation but had never been adequately fulfilled. Among these tasks were the responsibilities for "planning" and for "looking ahead" to long-term national needs. There was, in brief, an expressed need for something (as yet undefined) called a national science policy. One of the Congress's motivations in fostering this charge was to render this portion of the President's staff, which had up until that time been unavailable to the Congress, more accessible and accountable to public (i.e., congressional) scrutiny and questioning.

The other feature that was subject to a marked shift in the early 1960s was a broadening of the agenda of concerns and issues for the Office of the Science Adviser from almost purely military ones to a much expanded series of domestic issues. Presidents and their staffs generally sought scientific and technical advice on questions of military preparedness and national security. National priorities had begun to shift in the 1960s. Social issues of health and welfare, employment, and urban decay joined those of energy, transportation, and the integrity of the environment in vying for national and government attention. In corresponding fashion, the role of the presidential science advisory apparatus was broadened to accommodate this shift. In the immediate sense, the shift was a result of an increasing difficulty which Wiesner experienced in trying to assist the President on national security matters. McGeorge Bundy, as special assistant for national security, had assumed a larger role than had his predecessors, and the staff of the National Security Council was enlarged. In addition, there evolved a series of specialized if ad hoc White House advisory offices on national issues, each with a substantial scientific component. Beginning in the 1960s, there arose a National Aeronautics and Space Council and a National Council on Marine Resources and Engineering Development. The Atomic Energy Commission had been established some years earlier. (This trend continued into the 1970s with the creation of a Federal Energy Office and the establishment of a Council on Environmental Policy in the Executive Office.)

This broadening of activities of the science adviser and his staff together with establishment of other related agencies in the Executive Office has been seen by some as contributing to a weakening of the functions and influence of the Science Adviser.[12] What perhaps is yet unclear is whether the "weakening" was simply due to bureaucratic competitiveness, whether it accrued from an intrinsic inability of hard science to deliver useful ideas and solutions to "soft" domestic and social issues, or whether it came principally from President Johnson's antipathy toward scientists.

Eleven years later, in 1973, President Nixon provoked a new rearrangement (or disarrangement) of the presidential science advisory apparatus—again through a reorganization plan.[13] The arrangements solidified in 1962 had given the Science Adviser four interrelated roles. He was, first of all, the President's science advisor—a function in which he served formally in the White House as a counsellor to the President. He was chairman of the President's Science Advisory Committee—a group of eighteen to twenty persons who met formally for two days each month. Associated with the PSAC organization was an assemblage of approximately two hundred consultants whose counsel and judgment were sought when they served as members of PSAC panels. Thirdly, he was chairman of the Intragovernmental Federal Council on Science and Technology. Finally, he was the director of his own staff—formally known as the Office of Science and Technology. This latter position was, strictly speaking, a part of the Executive Office of the President. In practice, this distinction meant that the Congress could summon the director to testify with his Executive Office hat but not the science adviser with his White House title.

The changes brought about in 1973 amounted to a translation of some functions and an abolition of others. The title and most of the functions of science adviser were handed to Dr. H. Guyford Stever who also served as the director of the government agency, the National Science Foundation. Importantly in this new setting, the science adviser was relieved of his responsibilities for defense and security issues. The President's Science Advisory Committee was abolished while the Federal Council on Science and Technology was retained. Finally, a new staff office was created to take the place of the Office of Science and Technology.

The Nixon reorganization proposal evoked effectively no opposition in the Congress and, in the immediate term, none of the cries of anguish and surprise that one might have anticipated from the academic and scientific communities. Professional and scientific groups, however, did eventually mobilize themselves in ways which were effective in lobbying the Congress for their eventual return to the White House. The National Academy of Sciences proffered a report in 1974 which recommended a role for scientists in presidential policy making and offered a plan which included three scientific counsellors.[14] Former science advisers, individual scientists and engineers, and spokesmen for professional societies all urged on the Congress the point of view that it was in the best interest of both the nation and the President to have good scientific and technical advice formally and institutionally available at his right hand.[15]

A number of legislative proposals were put forward. Finally, in May 1976, the National Science and Technology Policy, Organization and Priorities Act of 1976 was enacted into law—giving the presidential science advisory apparatus a congressionally initiated statutory basis for the first time.[16] This new law established the position and the functions of the science adviser; it charged him with developing and fostering a "national science policy"; it gave him responsibilities for coordinating federal scientific activities and provided him with a new intragovernmental coordinating committee. The new law did not name a single, visible advisory committee of part-time advisers (to replace the former President's Science Advisory Committee). Most significantly, the science adviser was given specific functions in relation to national security affairs and in relation to the federal budgeting process—perhaps the most important of the pieces of leverage he was to possess in articulating with the governmental processes. The Congress was careful to reserve an element of accountability to themselves. The new law obliged the writing of an annual report on the state of science and technology and a periodically revised five-year outlook for science and technology. Finally, the Congress charged the science adviser with the development and articulation of explicit "National Science Policy."[17]

Once again, science and technology were assumed to be of potential value to major domestic challenges in areas of health, transportation, social welfare, and environment. The Congress accepted the urgings of those scientists and engineers who had insisted that there was positive national gain to be realized from the making of scientific and technical advice available to the President for major national policy issues. Killian, himself, speaking in 1974 as the chairman of the National Academy of Sciences' Ad Hoc Panel on Science Policy, declared that "the proposal we make, the instrument which we describe, is not in our minds an advocacy group for science. We propose an instrument to share in national policy making."[18]

*Analysis for Priority Setting: Past Failures
and Present Need*

Killian's and others' proposal that it is in the President's and the nation's interest to have good scientific advice and judgment available to aid in policy making assumes certain key features about governmental processes. The proposal assumes that there is in place a reasonably orderly process dedicated to the establishment of national objectives and to the analysis of optional strategies for achieving those objectives. It assumes, of course even before this stage, that there is a political *desire* to undertake this orderly process. Finally, implicit in all of this, is an assumption that such an exercise should have some element of forward thinking or future orientation—to allow it to do more than simply react hastily to the never-ending series of crises brought to the government.

There had indeed been serious attempts at evolving explicit and analytic attempts at policy making. Most of these have been coupled to the government budgeting process. There have been many admonitions to apply the skills of systems analysis and operations research to governmental planning for domestic policies and programs. Planning, Programming, and Budgeting (PPBS) achieved what was considered utility, if not success, in the Department of Defense in the early 1960s. Advocates of PPBS urged its translation into the domestic agencies beginning in 1965. In the early and mid-1970s, a structured process known as Management by Objectives was imposed upon the federal budgeting processes for domestic programs. Currently, the budget-setting functions are governed by yet another structured system—Zero Based Budgeting. In addition, in recent years a good deal of attention has been focused on the application of mathematical modeling techniques—both to simulate and to project for large, complex domestic issues. The underlying notion in each of these cases was that one could articulate goals and propose objectives. By careful study and analysis, one could arrange programs and expenditures in a ranked or priority fashion and then act on the results of those analyses. In spite of the logic behind these planning and budgeting tools, in spite of the basic soundness of some of the methods, these instruments and methods have generally not been eagerly adopted and embraced by the public policy machinery.

In the first approximation, systematic methods for establishing priorities, and for sorting through alternative pathways to the achievement of national goals, would seem to represent a substantial improvement over less systematic methods. Charles Schultze, former Budget Bureau director and now chairman of the Council of Economic Advisers, was one of the most enthusiastic spokesmen for PPBS. He claimed as advantages of PPBS:

1. Careful identification of goals and activities in governmental processes.
2. Analysis of output of a given program in terms of its objectives.
3. Measurement of total program costs for not one but several years into the future.
4. Formulation of objectives and progress extending beyond a single year of the annual budget submission.
5. Establishment of analytic procedures as a systematic part of the budget review.[19]

Schultze argued in favor of special analysis for decision making in the domestic arena because of what he saw as the fast-rising proportion of government spending for domestic programs. In 1968, when he urged the use of PPBS, he pointed to the fact that the federal budget for civilian programs had risen from less than 1 percent of the GNP in the 1920s to 5 percent after World War II and to nearly 10 percent in 1968. Interestingly, if a national health insurance scheme were to be enacted, health alone among domestic matters would account for approximately 10 percent of the federal budget by 1980.[20]

In spite of the apparent logic of these arguments, in spite of what may appear as compelling arguments in behalf of systematic, forward-looking, and explicit analysis for priority setting and budgeting, PPBS did not survive. Neither has there been any other recognized vehicle or established methodology for assisting public administrators (including the President) to formulate national policies and programs. It is against this background that the science advisory apparatus is placed. Specifically, it is the absence of any suitable analytic process in the White House for developing policy objectives and options that makes impossible or difficult the science adviser's task of contributing to the policy process.

Historically, the leadership of the scientific community viewed its role in science policy conservatively. Assistance to the President in sorting out priorities among purely scientific ventures or decisions on how much federal money should be spent for research and development represent the boundaries of "science policy" with which scientists have traditionally felt comfortable. The grand plan to couple scientific and technical knowledge through research and education to the agricultural sector of the nation in the nineteenth century had been the brainchild of politicians, not of scientists.[21] Without question, the OSRD, and through it the scientific establishment, had made very tangible contributions to the national project, victory in World War II. However, that momentum, that willingness to contribute to broad policy decisions in the company of other interests, such as economists and politicians, did not persist following the war. Among other things, the original legislation establishing the National Science Foundation in 1950 charged that body with developing a "national science policy." In fact, it had been intended by some that the NSF would assume a lead role within the federal government through coordination and representation of scientific activities. Instead, the NSF chose to view its science policy role very narrowly. As late as 1960, its director, Dr. Alan Waterman, defined science policy as the policy governing the support for research (and, perhaps, development).[22] It was understandable, in these terms, that Dr. Waterman, in reflecting on the first ten years of the National Science Foundation, considered that "national policy for science is a matter primarily to be determined by the scientists themselves."[23]

With time, however, there grew a number of advocates of the point of view that scientists and engineers did have a useful contribution to make to the public policy machinery for domestic issues. The implications of their recommendations were that a number of large, important decisions were made by the government in which a scientific and technical component was important and prominent. Appropriate judgments in these cases depended upon the availability of good technical advice. There was a role for scientists to contribute *actively* alongside others—other advocates and detractors with vested interests in the outcomes.

Again, in the instances in which a recommendation was made in behalf of this type of contribution, there was assumed to be a place for systematic planning and analysis for domestic issues and programs. The Report of the National Commission on Technology, Automation, and Economic Progress observed in 1966:

We are concerned with *how* we decide what to choose. Congress has asked us "How can human and community needs be met?" But there is a prior question: "How can they be more readily recognized and agreed upon?"

What concerns us is that we have no such ready means for agreement, that such decisions are often made piecemeal with no relation to each other, that vested interests are often able to obtain unjust shares, and that few mechanisms are available which allow us to see the range of alternatives and thus enable us to choose with a comprehension of the consequences of our choices.[24]

The Commission saw the strengthening and making more orderly the processes of forecasting and analysis for decision making in an increasingly technological and complex society as major, or even imperative challenges. However, even as they recommended the use of systems analysis as an aid to planning, the commission members recognized the basic strengths of government as a reflection of public desires:

The basic decisions on policy, of course, are made by the President and the Congress operating within the framework of constitutional processes and individual liberties as interpreted by the courts. And this system has been the political main stay of a free society. Our concern is to strengthen this system at a time when social and technological change begins to confront us so directly and when we need some means of assessing the consequences of such changes in a comprehensive way.[25]

Still others saw something broader and more meaningful politically in the phrase, national science policy. In the legislative deliberations of 1961, concerned with science organization and the President's office, a subcommittee staff study spoke of the "President's Problem"—a need for valid and usable scientific advice in his tasks of sorting through competing options and programs of a variety of sorts.[26] It was anticipated that a new, fully staffed office in the White House would help the President "look ahead." The principal expressed concern was for programs and activities of a military and national security nature. However, among the advantages listed by those advocating the acceptance of the Reorganization Plan No. 2 in 1962 was that of an agency with authority in the area of across-the-board forward planning.[27] The Reorganization Plan, itself, explicitly charged the Science Adviser with an "assessment of selected scientific and technical developments and programs in relation to their impact on national policies."[28] Here was indeed a very different role than one of simply considering how monies for the furtherance of science were best allocated among various categories of research.

By the early 1970s, scientists and engineers had become public advocates for a formal role and an institutionalized mechanism to bring scientific and technical advice to bear on the judgments and deliberations for large domestic issues of housing, health, transportation and social welfare. A Preinaugural Panel on Science and Technology in late 1968 had clearly outlined a series of pressing domestic issues, including health care and the environment, where scientists and science had something to offer. That panel recommended that the incoming President grant cabinet status to the President's science adviser and create a Council of Scientific Advisers. The tone of the introductory statement is revealing:

In times of national emergency, as in the world wars, science and technology have been mobilized and effectively utilized. The Panel believes the Federal Government should utilize scientists and engineers much more effectively in the current environmental crises, in the provision of education and health care to the people, and in the social crises of the cities.[29]

In 1969, the White House invited the advice of a "President's Task Force on Science Policy." The effort was one of a series of study task forces put in place that year to demonstrate presidential interest in a variety of subjects. Its chairman, Ruben Mettler, in his letter to the President accompanying the final report, urged that this was a "time of unusual need and unusual reward for Presidential leadership in bringing the tools of science and technology more effectively to bear on critical social, urban, and environmental problems, as part of a broader program to properly relate science policy to the Nation's goals and purposes."[30] The report itself was even more forthright in stating that "national policy governing science and technology should in principle, be a mirror image of our national goals and purposes."[31]

At roughly the same time, a Panel on Science and Technology Policy of the President's Science Advisory Committee was studying the kinds of organizational improvements that could be made in bringing scientific advice to bear on policy making at the presidential level. Notably, that panel considered it essential that the science and technology advisory mechanism adopt a "more policy oriented role."[32]

The same theme was amplified during the later deliberations over the question of a statutory basis for the presidential science adviser. The congressional committees which proposed restoring the Science Adviser to his White House location after 1973 were more forthright in their recognition of this need to consider science and technology—not by themselves but in the mainstream of economic, social, and national security issues. Those witnesses who testified before the Congress frankly stated the importance of long-range policy research and analysis of which science and technology were important components. An unsolicited NAS report to the House Committee on Science and Technology in 1974 concluded that "science and technology can fully serve the federal government—and the nation," but only if adequate organizational changes are made in the President's office to accommodate a source of scientific and technological analysis and judgment.*[33]

Here, indeed, were scientists talking about the "President's problem." The world was increasingly complex. The time constants for decision making were increasingly foreshortened. Big decisions about big and important programs invariably had substantial technical components. The President needed scientifically trained experts to help him make these decisions. Scientists were capable of that role and were willing to help.

The most cynical, of course, saw this move on the part of scientists as simply a different form of advocacy. That is, in the face of a somewhat more critical political view of federal budgets for the performance of research, and in the face of an "exile" of scientists from the White House structure, some suggested that this was an inevitable tack by a special interest trying to reestablish its claim on the political process. There was, too, a new brand of ambivalence among the scientists. The problem now was that science would promise too much. That is, in their zeal to appear to be "useful" to society, scientists would foster a public image of a scientific machine which

---

*Interestingly, this report, whose chairman was James Killian, did not proceed as far as one of its members, Donald Rice, had recommended. Rice, then the president of the Rand Corporation, and formerly an assistant director of the Office of Management and Budget, had foreseen the strong need for broad analysis in reaching informal judgments at the Presidential level. He, as did others, called for the establishment of some sort of a formal mechanism for analysis in the Executive Office as a necessary requisite to bringing scientific advice to bear on policy decisions. Donald B. Rice, "Scientific and Technical Capability of OMB Staff." Background paper prepared for the ad hoc Committee on Science and Technology, National Academy of Sciences, Washington, D. C., 2 March 1974 (unpublished).

inevitably could not deliver on its implied promises.* Symptomatic, perhaps, of their ambivalence, Philip Handler, president of the National Academy of Sciences, in testimony to the Congress, acknowledged in cursory fashion the importance of long-range policy research and analytic capability in the Executive Office, but suggested that the academy (Killian) committee "had no informed opinion" as to how to make it a reality.[34]

However, there was a new frame of mind. One version of the National Science, Engineering, and Technology Policy and Organization Act of 1975 declared that the President's office should establish and maintain "central policy planning elements."[35] It was in this setting that science for governmental and national needs was to make its contribution. As a first step, even before a new science advisory apparatus was approved by the Congress, the President's office engaged a "planning" effort of a series of outside experts to provide guidance for a new office. This series of two advisory groups was designed to guide in the "wise use of science and technology in achieving important national objectives. One was to examine the contribution of technology to economic strength and the other was concerned with new advances in science and technology.[36]

Factors That Discourage Analysis for Policy Making

The case for deliberate and dedicated analysis for the purposes of policy consideration and decision seems compelling and logical. Yet, in spite of the logic expressed by its advocates, there has been remarkably little success in bringing systematic explicit methods of analysis to bear on the domestic policy process. PPBS did not survive as an instrument of public decision making for domestic governmental programs; nor is there any other vehicle or established methodology for assisting public administrators (including the President) to formulate national policies and programs.

Why is it that the explicit statement of objectives, the systematic establishment of priorities, and the analytic sorting of alternative pathways to those goals are received with essentially no enthusiasm? There are perhaps two principal reasons. On the one hand, the use of explicit and systematic methods by government clashes with the traditional, public consensus patterns of democratic decision making. The other reason is an "internal"

---

*The debate among the biomedical scientific community over the emerging National Cancer Program was perhaps one of the best illustrations of this ambivalence.

political one which relates to the relative amount of bargaining power held at any point in time by the President versus the legislature.

Charles Lindblom was perhaps the one most clearly identified with criticism of the use of Planning, Programming, and Budgeting in political decision making. Lindblom maintained that there was an important and inherent conflict between the traditional, advocacy-related, consensus formulation of public decisions and the analytic and studied attempt to make objectives explicit and to analyze alternative means of reaching them. It is Lindblom's contention that the integrity and efficiency of consensus building and decisions through advocacy (which he maintains is the only way to reach "good" decisions) is threatened precisely by encouraging debate on objectives. Goals, in Lindblom's view, should not receive specific attention as such attention renders consensus more rather than less difficult to reach.[37] Decisions through advocacy and public consensus, in Lindblom's litany "the science of muddling through," are, in his view, an absolutely essential element in democratic decision making.[38]

One could add at this point that the Lindblom view is strongly held by those who occupy contemporary political office. Among the many results of this pattern of political thinking was the attempt to propose "national goals" by a presidentially appointed National Goals Research Staff. The final product, *Toward Balanced Growth: Quantity with Quality*,[39] was so thoroughly diluted by the time of its publication that it was totally incapable of provoking any novel idea in the public's mind. There is every indication that those in political office who started the national goals research effort found themselves with a project whose initiation they thoroughly regretted.

One rejoinder to the Lindblom point of view (and one expressed by Charles Schultze, for example) is that the advocacy process itself would be measurably strengthened by becoming a more informed advocacy process. All parties would benefit, so goes the argument, by arming the various points of view with good analysis and good information.

Fundamental to this nation's concern for explicit objective setting and forward planning for establishing a political agenda are perhaps three closely related phenomena. One is a long-standing and deep-seated distrust of anything that borders on national economic planning.[40] A second is simply the striking heterogeneity of interests (and "special interests") for which this nation is notable. This heterogeneity is, of course, a source of enormous richness and strength and, at the same time, a basis for great divisiveness. The third, which in a way sets off the other two in even bolder relief, is the recent trend toward more openness in government.

The historian Robert Wiebe has explored at length the finely divided character of the American nation in his provocative essay *The Segmented Society*.[41] For Wiebe, segmentation of America into community groups, professional groups, economic interests, etc., began early in the nation's history and continues to be the dominant force shaping the national political scene for purely domestic issues. Wiebe observed that "a segmented society with its special aversion to disorder charged politics with a particularly broad and basic range of responsibilities, a set of commandments to preserve liberty within the compartments while maintaining a common society among them."[42] Grand visions and broad purposes expressed by presidents have been frustrated and rendered futile from the earliest days of the republic. Government is expected to maintain, not to step out in front of major national issues.

What politics expressed, government reflected. Over the centuries the most useful image of government was that of an empty vessel, a container into which power flowed and formed but which provided nothing of its own.[43]

Planning in that setting, almost by definition, could never be a palatable, high-level governmental activity. With the passage of decades of history, Wiebe reminds us, the federal government and its President have increasingly assumed the role of presiding over an "elaborate scheme of brokerage."[44] The burdens of maintenance have been increased with time.

Again, what has been described here applies in particular (if not exclusively) to national domestic issues. In contrast to its preoccupation with regional and economic national interests, the electorate has shown itself repeatedly to be quite willing to defer to its government for essentially all of the issues involved in defense and national security.

The opening of the details of government to public viewing in recent years has further accentuated this phenomenon. A new awareness of what government is doing and even thinking *in behalf of* its citizenry has risen out of a period of national anxiety over what government is thinking and doing *to* its citizens. "Sunshine" and freedom of information are the particular windows of the moment through which public scrutiny pours. My point is not to render a value judgment about whether the doing of government in public is good or bad. It is certainly true, as Theodore Lowi declared nearly a decade ago, that participatory democracy is administratively more cumbersome.[45] My only point, however, is that the segmentation of our society into a myriad of special interests and a general national concern for maintaining immediate and stable conditions among the segments combine with openness in government to further constrain any solely rational and analytically based judgments about domestic futures.

In addition to the view from the outside (that of the electorate), there is the equally important "view from the inside" of government. In Richard Neustadt's description of the government as "separate institutions sharing powers" the effective influence of a President accrues from three sources: (1) the bargaining advantage inherent in his job with which he persuades other men to enact his expectations by what their own responsibilities require them to do; (2) the expectations of those other men regarding his ability and will to use the various advantages they think he has; and (3) the estimates of those men as to how the President's public views him and how the public would view them if they follow his bidding.[46]

It may be assumed (or Congress would assume) that if the President were to establish an effective and adequately staffed "Office of Analysis and Planning," he would pose a threat to the existing balance of power in at least two ways. First, by arming himself with the necessary resources to reach systematic conclusions about national goals and priorities, he would thereby increase his share of influence and leverage over decisions in excess of that exercised by the Congress and by outside interest groups. Secondly, it may be expected that the President would deliberately use these augmented resources in various ways, not only for the performance of their substantive functions, but for increasing the "effectiveness" of his leadership and for magnifying his bargaining influence relative to all others having a voice in national management. Among the "separate institutions sharing power," the President's share would be increased relative to that wielded by others.*

The net result of all of this is that politically driven administrators (at all levels of government) do not find it to their advantage to engage in explicit planning for policy making. They find it incompatible with the rewards of their office to put in place an analytic and planning exercise in close proximity to their office. Those few elements of planning and analysis which do exist are characteristically and carefully kept at arm's length from the policy maker himself. The process of looking into the future, if done with care and rigor, and the data and the methods of projecting, if valid, inevitably raise red flags or threatening signals for some part of the electorate. The implied threat is that of rearrangement of some part of national life with seemingly favorable impacts on some segments and unfavorable effects on others. If the nation is to take seriously a desire for relative independence from foreign sources of petroleum, it may be obliged to dig more deeply into its own resources—offshore and onshore. An explicit policy to augment the

---

*The evolution in recent years of the Office of Technology Assessment and the Congressional Budget Office are, perhaps, examples of this phenomenon.

production of agricultural products could have implications for population shifts, transportation needs, and industries that compete with agriculture for land.

In each case, a perceptive electorate or its representatives will see certain threatening possibilities to long-term growth or to continued and stable well-being. In some cases, merely having it known that a "plan" or analysis is being considered makes it uncomfortable for an administrator as he becomes suspect or the target of criticism from his political adversaries. One of the accommodations to the phenomenon has been to maintain the terms of such planning activities secret. Another, more common, route is simply not to engage in the exercise at all and keep planning far away from "the house." In many ways, this is one of the most discouraging factors. In spite of the imperative for long-range (or even short-range) planning due to the size, complexity and the pronounced technological character of national programs, along with the large impacts and expenditures they imply, planning of this sort is not a luxury which the "system" has encouraged or permitted. The exceptions have been those instances such as war, national security, depression, and the national space program for which a national consensus was easily available.*

This phenomenon is not confined to the White House or Executive Office. Neither is it an entirely new phenomenon. One of the interesting and well-documented accounts of this matter concerns a group of social scientists and economists who were brought together in the 1920s in the service of agriculture. The Bureau of Agricultural Economics was created in 1922 as a focus for some of the nation's best economists, demographers, and other social scientists. Its immediate patron and client was the secretary of agriculture. Its aim was to bring some of the finest academic talent to bear on nonacademic problems such as profitability and productivity of agriculture. The scientists called together in that office were part of a group who became known as "service intellectuals"—persons well respected by their peers in academic departments who were willing and even eager to apply their talents to real and important problems of national life.

The Bureau of Agricultural Economics of U.S.D.A. was given a much augmented charter in 1933 with the passage in that year of the Agricultural

*In fairness, it must be admitted that, at any point in time, there is inevitably a certain amount of ambivalence toward planning in government. The abolition of the National Resources Planning Board was followed by the enactment of the Full Employment Act which constituted the Council of Economic Advisers. In the midst of continuing anti-planning sentiments, Congress itself established the Congressional Budget Office and the Office of Technology Assessment.

Adjustment Act (the Christgau bill). This new law thrust the national government squarely into the practical and immediate problems then facing agriculture in a way that up to that time was unknown. There was, of course, a crisis of that moment comparable to that of a war. The depression gave the President and his government a charter in favor of national mobilization in kind.

The new law called for agricultural production control and marketing agreements. Planning for appropriate land use was suddenly a legitimate activity and the government appropriated a sum of money to assist in the withdrawal of submarginal land. Most important, the Department of Agriculture was given a congressional charter to establish the administrative machinery needed to build a program of national planning. The Bureau of Agricultural Economics was made the central, analytical, and intellectual instrument responsible for that planning.

In time, the Bureau of Agricultural Economics was, in a sense, eminently successful in its mission. In fact, it was too successful and was eventually put out of business because it had performed its intended job only too well. There were inevitably different factions within the agricultural community who received the government's thinking about agricultural futures differently. While there were some strong supporters, there arose some overwhelming detractors.

There did indeed develop some blurring of the roles of analysis and planning with action and management. Yet, the bureau began with perhaps a stronger commission for meaningful, action-oriented government programs than ever before. In any case, there developed great divisions of opinion among farm leaders and businessmen.

The Bureau of Agricultural Economics in 1935 turned its sights toward the lot of agriculture in the South where cotton had been king. The social scientists quickly became aware of growing problems of land tenancy, of emerging racial conflicts, of problems related to the use of migrant labor, and of migration away from the rural landscape. When these red flags were raised, they provoked a storm of protest.

Most important, the bureau economists foresaw a declining market for cotton. They recognized that government efforts to maintain cotton prices at high levels would eventually drive American cotton out of the world market. As a result, the economists evolved a series of plans to accommodate the dilemma and ease the dependency of the South away from the exclusiveness of the cotton based economy. It was hoped that many farmers eventually would be encouraged to move out of cotton production. Economic incentives were developed to encourage agricultural diversity of replacement of some agriculture with industrialization.

As Kirkendall, who has documented this story in great detail, noted, the criticism of this Cotton Conversion Program developed "at least as rapidly as support for it."[47] This opposition combined with outrage over a fact-finding survey performed by some of the bureau's sociologists of race relations and class structure (the Coahoma County Affair). Even some of the basic statistical work brought troubles for the bureau. Congress accused the bureau of "misbehaving" when its economists supplied the Office of Price Administration with factual information which the latter office used as a basis for the 1946 cotton price ceiling.

Members of Congress were outraged. Members of the executive were embarrassed. The fact that the government would even contemplate the possibility of ultimate conversion from cotton and would look into broad social implications of programs aroused the organized ire of agricultural pressure groups and drew condemnation from members of Congress.

The bureau was prohibited from conducting social surveys and from doing agricultural planning. Research administrators who accepted the challenge to deal explicitly with real problems and to assist in the matters of policy making and planning found themselves severely attacked. In fact, their negative rewards seemed to bear a direct relationship to the quality of their effort. The better the quality and the fuller the research effort for agricultural policies, the greater the political penalties that were ultimately visited upon the administrators. Economic research received its greatest support at times when agriculture and farmers were undergoing the most stress and change. One other problem which arose was an ever present conflict between policies aimed at benefiting the farmer and those directed toward a broader "national interest." (This, of course, implies that the two are not necessarily the same.) During the course of the history of the Bureau of Agricultural Economics, those administrators who stood aside from their current problems made little impact. Those who devoted the research efforts of the department to "safe" areas, isolated from programs and policies, had little influence on its policies or programs.

The development of a source of data and a strong and competent analytic capacity in close proximity to policy makers inevitably proved threatening to others who wished to control the "information." Thus, it was in the interest of advocate or pressure groups, in the sense of preserving their bargaining power, to keep the government relatively uninformed.

In 1953, the Bureau of Agricultural Economics was abolished and its functions were distributed to other sections of the Department of Agriculture but were purposely placed two steps removed from the secretary of agriculture. In 1964, upon his resignation as director of agricultural economics, Willard Cochrane contended that the Economic Research Service had no congressional backing for its appropriations, since it enjoyed no constituency. Many congressmen would oppose it unless its research results turned out "right" and its fate would inevitably be uncertain without the very strong backing of a secretary of agriculture.[48]

Thus, the major problem is not the technical hurdle of predicting futures, but instead the challenge, above all, is to make the products of analysis and forecasting politically palatable. The experience to date shows that as the processes of systematic analysis and prediction become better and better, they may become correspondingly less and less politically attractive.

3. NATIONAL HEALTH POLICY

Background

I t is difficult to know where to place a beginning in discussing the historical underpinnings of governmental health policy in the United States. Health care in America has traditionally been a mixed private-public blessing—historically, more private than public. The Commission on the Costs of Medical Care had delivered its final report in 1932.[1] The principal recommendations of that commission—medicine should be organized around group practice together with health insurance or prepayment for services—were essentially the same recommendations that were to be offered by commissions and task forces for the next forty years. One of the findings emphasized by that massive, five-year-long commission was that medical care was highly unevenly distributed across the United States—leaving rural America remarkably underserved.

As David Mechanic was to observe much later, in one sense American medicine was remarkably receptive to experimentation and innovation, especially of a scientific and technical character. However, in contrast to countries such as Great Britain, widespread adoption of social change was met with great resistance.[2] Medicine in America was entrepreneurial, and its practitioners considered independence of thought and action to be of the utmost importance. But then those terms characterized essentially all other major American activities. Independent, individualized forms of medical practice had been common to almost all other parts of the industrialized world but with time, were supplanted by state financed and often state organized and managed systems in many cases. In these terms, the United States became a setting for an extraordinary amount of social experimentation. At any one point in time, the combined patterns of private care and public intervention represented a complex mosaic of trials and demonstrations of diffused systems of financing, groupings of physicians and institutions and organizations. Some, like the Blue Cross organization or the Kaiser Permanente system, were born out of a locally felt desire to cover an unmet need. Others were the product of government initiative—using the leverage of monies raised through general taxes and an expressed popular mandate through congressional action to "do something" to effect improvement in the health care system. Perhaps the most remarkable aspect of this history is the fact that the national debate over how bad or good the health system is and what might or ought to be done to improve it has continued for such a prolonged period of time.

One common denominator of essentially all of the public and governmental discussion about health has been the cost of providing health care. The massive, self-generated commission begun in 1927 was termed the Commission on the *Costs* of Medical Care. The totality of the national expenditures in 1929 for health care amounted to $3.65 billion. In that year, such a sum represented four percent of the gross national product. Clearly, this question of costs was a major underlying concern which led to the establishment of the commission. However, the commission concluded that the level of expenditures was not out of line in the perspective of other public and private expenditures.* The terms of the concern were interesting. In spite of what was considered to be a large national expenditure, health care was very unevenly distributed, with a distinct lack of it available to those with lower incomes. At the same time, incomes of practitioners themselves, which accounted at that time for 40 percent of the total health bill, were of concern because in many cases they were too *low* or were very uneven.†[3]

By the late 1960s, there were increasingly heard concerns about a "crisis in health." The dimensions of the crisis were not always well defined. In part, these concerns were part of a general pattern of national desire for improvement in the social welfare fabric of the nation. The country had matured and had developed economically to the extent that it could afford to direct some of its attention to matters of poverty and problems of underserved or especially impacted segments of society. In its self-examination, the country found imbalances in the distribution of wealth and opportunities to seek wealth. The 1960s became the preeminent period in recent times to redress

---

*The commission's report compared the total national health expenditures in the midst of the depression to a larger total national spending for "tobacco, toilet articles and recreation." *Medical Care for the American People*, p. 13.
†It was estimated that, in 1929, over half the general practitioners of the nation had net incomes of less than $2,500.

some of these imbalances through the tools of education, job training, and the provision of social services—including health.

The major public concerns for health revolved around cost of health care and problems of accessibility to health care for persons who sought it. National expenditures for health care in 1950 amounted to $12 billion. This sum represented 4.6 percent of the GNP—not substantially different from the pattern in 1929. By 1968, health care expenditures were $53.1 billion and claimed almost 7 percent of the GNP.* The rate of increase of these expenditures was as striking as was their absolute value. The fraction of the total accounted for by professional fees was by now only 15 percent. An enormous part of the increase was attributed to hospitals and all that went into them and to rapidly rising costs of labor. Between 1950 and 1968, while the Consumer Price Index rose 45 percent, hospital costs rose 171 percent *relative* to the CPI.[4]

A number of factors contributed to this striking picture. One was simply general inflation. Another was a general increase in demand for health care services by members of the public—due in part to an increase in the capacity of clinical medicine to give diagnostic insight and, to a lesser extent, to provide therapeutic relief for disease. Coupled with this was a generally rising expectation by members of the public as to what medicine could do.[5] In part, this increase in expenditures related to a change in the "product" of clinical medicine. In latter years, this product had become more complex, more scientifically based, both more technologically encumbered and more labor intensive, and therefore, more expensive. The growth in numbers of nonphysician or ancillary personnel in medicine increased enormously. On the average, while the percentage of physicians to all other health care personnel was 30 percent in 1910, it was 9.6 percent in 1970.[6]

The mixture of health care problems—disease entities and injuries and the contributors to mortality—had, of course, changed over the years. Mortality from all causes had declined steadily from the beginning of the century until the mid-1950s. Prominent causes of death early in the century, particularly infectious disease, had been replaced by cardiovascular disease, chronic degenerative diseases (including cancer), and accidents. Longevity increased and an increasingly aged population, by itself, meant a larger universe of people "available" to be affected by chronic degenerative processes.

During the 1960s, the federal government had inserted itself in several ways into what had essentially been a private sector. The traditional place of

---

*As a further note to this continuing history, national health care expenditures in 1977 amounted to $162.6 billion or 8.8 percent of the GNP.

the federal government had been to underwrite medical research and to provide certain, direct health care services to specific groups, such as veterans, military personnel, and merchant seamen, for whom it was felt the state had a special obligation. The principal change in the federal role came in 1965 with the enactment of Medicare and Medicaid in behalf of the elderly and the impoverished.

Alongside the pressures to "do something" about the prices and costs of health care was an increasingly felt pressure to revise and to improve the form in which health services were provided or were available to consumers. It was evident to many that medical care had become (or continued to be) unevenly available—both geographically and across income classes. Some of this had come about by virtue of a marked geographical redistribution of the nation's population (including physicians) over a period of several decades—from rural America and small towns into cities and out again into suburban communities. In addition, the new financing schemes (Medicare and Medicaid), while partially satisfying unmet needs, themselves provoked additional demand.

Then, during the 1960s, there arose alongside the health care financing issues, a growing national concern about how to deliver the benefits of clinical medicine to communities of people. A number of experimental pilot and demonstration programs evolved whose general aim was to determine how better to design health care programs and services. Participation by both consumers and providers was accommodated. The two complementary federal health care demonstration programs of this period were the Regional Medical Program and the Comprehensive Health Care Planning Program.

Further, a prominent element in the federal health strategy of the 1960s was the attempt to accommodate special "target" groups through funds or direct services. The list of "categorical programs" eventually became a long one. Mental retardation, alcoholism, family planning, drug addiction, migrant labor, American Indians, children, and Cuban refugees were among those categories singled out for specific assistance.

These several factors converged toward the end of the decade of the 1960s and conspired to raise some fundamental questions about health, health care, public policies and programs designed nominally to improve and protect health, and about many of the elements of the traditional practice of medicine. However, the fundamental issue remained that of *costs* of health care. As Herman Somers was to observe a short time later, "it was the highly visible, widely felt, cost pressure initially generating only price complaints, that now more than any single stimulus had made public issues of virtually all elements in the organizing and financing of health care."[7]

Health: An Issue Ripe for Political Attention

A Pre-Inaugural Task Force on Health, under the chairmanship of Professor John Dunlop, turned its attention in late 1968 to key health issues to be considered by the new administration. The President-elect was urged to think of health as worthy of national (presidential) attention. The public's interest in health matters was said to be high. Health care was described as being "in great ferment."[8] The task force members were persuaded that it was in the nation's (and the President's) interest to include remarks about health in a State of the Union Message and to deliver a separate message on health to the Congress.

Chief among all of the issues as seen by the task force members was the enormous expenditures of monies made nationally in behalf of health but with uncertain return in terms of improvement in health. This was a theme that had already begun to evolve as a political issue and would emerge eventually in discussions of health care in essentially all industrialized nations. In spite of high rates of national spending for health, there were segments of the population who were manifestly underserved. The task force took particular note of this matter as well as of the fact that the United States lagged behind many other nations in the record of infant mortality and life expectancy.

In addition to these factors, the task force acknowledged the fact that the federal government had assumed, in the decade about to be completed, a much enlarged role in health care. The form of the government's pattern of intervention was as important as the fact. By the end of the 1960s there was already in place a mosaic of categorical health (and social welfare) programs each of which was directed toward the expressed needs of specific, target groups. The task force recommended that it was timely to take stock of the results of all of these programs before entering upon new ones. The question of what to do with the long list of uncoordinated, sometimes poorly planned, categorical health and social welfare programs later became an enormous dilemma for the federal government. Each program carried with it a promise of realizing improvement through the expenditures of federal funds and a constituency developed around each program to sustain it and to increase the amount of money spent in its behalf. Funds and time were seldom sufficient to fulfill the promises and expectations. In many cases, the nature of the problems that a program was designed to attack was simply not resolvable through federal intervention.*[9]

---

*One of the examples often cited in this regard was the Heart Disease, Cancer, and Stroke Program. The promise raised when this program was announced was that the

Perhaps the most striking and strident indictment of this pattern of government mischief of raising false public expectations through categorical programs and through the pattern of throwing money at social problems was to come two years later in Secretary Elliot Richardson's final report to the Department of Health, Education, and Welfare. In that report, he decried the political exploitation that led to "exaggerated promises, ill-conceived programs, over-advertised 'cures' for intractable ailments," ending inevitably in a crisis in expectations.[10]

The task force did devote attention to the question of medical education and medical manpower—both for physicians and for other health care professionals. There was a "generally accepted view" that the nation needed more health care professionals of all types. The Carnegie Commission on Higher Education would shortly publish its views on needs for professional manpower in medicine and dentistry.[11] The Carnegie Commission's report, which was available early to the administration in draft form, spoke to the need for expanding the number of physicians in training by 50 percent by the end of the 1980s.*[12] The Carnegie Commission relied heavily in its arguments on the low rank of the United States in life expectancy at birth and on rising expectations for health care among members of its citizenry. The clear implication of all of this was that a betterment in the general health indices of the nation would follow an increase in the number of health professionals in practice—a position that was to be seriously challenged in the next few years.†[13]

This question of need for medical manpower, especially physician manpower

---

establishment and funding of centers dedicated to the early diagnosis and treatment of these disease entities would lead to a greater proportion of *cures*. In fact, this expectation simply could not be fulfilled since there was insufficient fundamental understanding of the causes of these diseases, and hence, of the possible routes of meaningful therapeutic intervention.

*A part of the rationale for this recommendation was a statement made by Dr. Roger Egeberg who eventually became assistant secretary for health of HEW. The statement spoke to the need for 50,000 additional physicians. The administration, in turn, pointed to the Carnegie Commission report as a basis for increasing the enrollment of medical schools.

†It is interesting to note that at the time of the Flexner Report (which was, in fact, an earlier report to the Carnegie Foundation) in 1910 the number of actively practicing physicians in the United States was 171 per 100,000 population. The Flexner Report's conclusion was that at that time there was at least an adequate supply of physicians, and perhaps an excess. A comparison was drawn in the Flexner Report between the United States and Germany, pointing out that Germany had fewer physicians but that its citizens were probably no less healthy than were Americans. In 1968, the number of active physicians in the United States was 150 per 100,000—a situation not much different from that which existed in 1910.

was to be a prominent part of health policy deliberations for the next several years. The federal government was to embrace the common wisdom of the time and develop a program of financial incentives (capitation grants) to encourage medical schools to increase their numbers of graduates. Within no more than three years, however, the government would have second thoughts about this policy and begin to predict an excess of physicians in practice.

A final theme of the Pre-Inaugural Task Force was that of making the existing health care resources of the nation more efficient and productive. The President was not urged to mount new programs. Rather, the existing ones should be made to operate in a more orderly and coordinated fashion. Stability of government organization was urged rather than massive reorganization of departments and programs. The task force did recognize the importance of control over funds and recommended that the assistant secretary of health be given jurisdiction over Medicare and Medicaid monies. Beyond a few, modest organizational proposals, however, the task force did not propose drastic administrative changes.

Development of a National Health Strategy. The
Health Policy Review Group

The politically minded advisers to the President did agree that health was a worthy issue for presidential attention. The administration, in March 1970, had sent to the Congress a legislative proposal supporting the establishment of prepaid group practice forms of medical organizations ("Health Maintenance Organizations"). There were other, discrete announcements and actions during the first year and a half of the new administration as well. However, the timing appeared particularly ripe to assemble and announce a more comprehensive or coordinated series of government actions and decisions which, together, would be known as a "national strategy" for health. Such a combined national health strategy had not been afforded government-wide and presidential attention in recent years. In the first approximation, there appeared to be a number of opportunities for programs and policies and for government action combined with private initiative that would galvanize public and professional attention and would lead to improvements in health care and health. The challenge appeared to be to determine which of the many possible items were appropriate issues to consider and what governmental actions should be thought of.

The first step was to seek from the secretary of Health, Education, and Welfare the benefit of his department's thinking. Thus, there was a call for what became known as "health options." The White House requested from HEW a discussion of all of the possible issues and actions that should be considered for new initiatives, for government programs, for budgetary emphasis, and for legislative initiatives.

A memorandum in July 1970 to Secretary Elliot Richardson called for a "comprehensive analysis" of health options in preparation for legislative proposals for the 92d Congress. The memorandum, while not particularly well composed, did invite a very wide scope of thinking on what the government should do (or redo) in behalf of the nation's health. Budgetary implications were important and were to be noted but the various alternatives were not to be excluded from discussion and analysis simply because they would cost a lot of money.[14]

In one sense, the replies to this memorandum were extensive. Dr. Roger Egeberg, assistant secretary for health, put several committees to work. However, there appeared to be little critical judgment exercised over the process. The result, by the end of October, was an enormous stack of telephone-book size, stylized reports on a very large variety of health and health care challenges and problems. The quality of these reports was quite variable. The most general conclusions that one could discern from these documents were that:

1. The statistics relating to health status of Americans indicated improvement. However, there remained large disparities in these measures among various income groups, occupational categories, etc.
2. There were real problems with the health care "system." However, simple tinkering with the elements of the system would not be adequate to effect meaningful change.

Because of the very extended nature of the Health Options Study, and because it was accompanied by no useful critical distillation suitable for translation into public policy and programs, the Health Options Study was deemed to be not helpful. Accordingly, a second much more hurried, more tightly directed study was begun, this time by the Executive Office of the President itself. This exercise, eventually to be known as the Health Policy Review Group, was directed by Richard Nathan, an assistant director in the Office of Management and Budget. There were eleven other participants—drawn from HEW, the Council of Economic Advisers, the OEO, the Veterans Administration, OMB, the Office of Science and Technology, and from other parts of the White House. The charge to this group was quite explicit—to "develop a coherent framework for policy decisions in the field of health"—in the hope of deriving a combined national strategy for health. The particular terms of reference for the group were reasonably succinct:

1. An analysis describing the appropriate role for the federal government in the nation's health system.
2. Identification and description of mechanisms to carry out responsibilities appropriate to the federal government.
3. A simplified statement of the Family Health Insurance financing proposal.[15]

Perhaps the most demanding of the charges to this group was that its work had to be completed within three weeks.[16]

The Health Policy Review Group began its life on November 18, 1970, and was given three weeks to produce its final product. The final product was to be a decision paper for the President from which he (and others on his staff) would choose projects and ideas for a political strategy.

The initial meeting started from a position that there should be a "coherent set of principles" as a basis for a national health policy (later to be known as a National Health Strategy). The key elements chosen to highlight in this regard were prevention of disease and emphasis on making health care available broadly and efficiently.

A great deal of attention was devoted to the definition of an appropriate role for the federal government. This was important in defining which programs and expenditures should be highlighted. It was also important, of course, in setting this new group of governmental strategies apart from what had come before. In this regard, it was felt that an appropriate federal role was one of leadership and catalysis. The government should undertake those programs and actions which no other body could perform as well. Where the federal government does insert itself, it should, however, make use of the full leverage value of the expenditures made in behalf of health. Ironically, of course, the ultimately chosen plan would involve or propose as much federal "intervention" as had characterized the programs of preceding administrations. However, now there were to be different forms of intervention—national health insurance, direct federal subsidies to medical education, and a dedicated federal program designed to alter the pattern of delivery of care termed the Health Maintenance Organization.

The subjects considered during the next three weeks were sharply delimited. The HEW representatives were prone to pour forth a very long list of ideas and potential initiatives related to narcotic drugs, family planning, health education, nutrition, environment and health, and others. However, the chairman restricted the number of subjects for discussion. A few of the government agencies such as the Department of Defense and the Veterans Administration made special pleadings for consideration of particular programs or for the preservation of the status quo of what they considered to be important elements.

A principal element of this evolving "national strategy" was a program of national health insurance. Daniel Patrick Moynihan, then a counsellor on the White House staff, had already evolved and fostered a presidential position in favor of a guaranteed minimum income ("income policy") known as the Family Assistance Plan. The discussions of health insurance turned around proposals that would be complementary to the goals of the Family Assistance Plan, which would preserve what was believed to be the best of private initiative. An additional goal was to replace the Medicaid program with a more efficient, less costly, and presumably more equitable health insurance scheme. Three versions—all variations of a common pattern—were considered. All of these plans were designed to underwrite the same series of health care benefits with a variable amount of premium contribution determined by a family's income level. The major difference among the plans was the extent to which families contributed to the cost of the plans through fixed premiums or at the time of receiving care (through coinsurance or deductibles). Dr. Martin Feldstein of Harvard, then a consultant to the government, proposed the use of variable amounts of coinsurance according to the ability to pay.

One of the elements which the Office of Science and Technology attempted to inject into these discussions was a consideration of the relationship (or nonrelationship) between expenditures made in behalf of health and the health status of the nation. This was an issue that grew in importance with the enormous increase in national spending for health. The common (political) wisdom generally supported the notion that the more the country spent in behalf of its personal and collective health, the healthier its populace would be. In 1967, William H. Forbes, a member of the faculty of Harvard University School of Public Health, published a paper in which he explored analytically the relationship between national expenditures for health and health itself.[17] Interestingly, Forbes's motivation for publishing his analysis was the series of implied promises that accompanied one of the categorical programs of the time—the National Heart Disease, Cancer and Stroke Program. Forbes was seriously concerned and frankly incensed at what he understood to be a national commitment to improve health which he reasoned could simply not be fulfilled. Accordingly, in his language, he set out to examine the hypothesis that more money meant more health.

Forbes observed that longevity after the age of ten increased markedly in the United States from 1900 to 1950 but seemed to reach a plateau in 1954. He further observed that, when compared with twenty other countries that had a better record of longevity (average lifetime remaining after the age of ten years) than the United States for the years 1944 through 1964, the rate of increase in longevity per decade in the United States was exceeded by all of them for males, except West Germany. The average remaining lifetime for the United States had remained constant but its rank among nations had fallen sharply for males and slightly for females. (Figure 3.1.) Forbes's own conclusion from this analysis was that "in the United States there is no longer any significant relation between the money spent on health and the results achieved."[18]

In essence, of course, this was a fundamental indictment of a massive amount of public policy that had been put in place especially over the course of the previous decade and a half. Further, the explanations seemed, at least on the surface, reasonably straightforward. Admittedly, the measure of health —mortality or its obverse, longevity—was a crude surrogate. It could be argued that mortality is too crude a measure to assess the great variety of important results of clinical medicine such as the relief of pain, correction of deformities, the relief of anxiety, or the frank cure of infectious disease. Yet, this could not be the entire explanation, in view of the seemingly large divergence between input and output and in view of the increasing rate of divergence. There are sound reasons for putting more reliance on mortality statistics than on morbidity records. Further, although mortality may be a crude index, one was still left with the problem of explaining a period of relatively fixed or, in the case of men, worsening mortality rates.

The major reasons to explain this finding, at least on the surface, seemed reasonably straightforward (although, perhaps, they appeared to run counter to the grain of common wisdom). One concern is the fact that prominent contributors to morbidity and mortality reflect environmental forces and social habits broadly speaking. Accidents (including automobile accidents linked to alcohol consumption) are among the ten leading causes of death in contemporary American life. Lung cancer and other forms of respiratory illness—strongly linked to cigarette smoking—have risen steadily in importance so as to reach epidemic proportions. The trends in national longevity, including those considered by Forbes, were to be reinforced through an analysis by the National Center for Health Statistics of causes of mortality in the 1960s.[19] This analysis noted that the long-term fall in overall death rates in the United States, characteristic of the first half of the twentieth century, leveled off in the 1950s. For males, the curve showed signs of beginning to rise. The National Center for Health Statistics examined the diseases that were responsible for this "excess mortality"—excess, that is, over the previously established trend. Eight categories of cause of death showed percentage increases in 1967 compared with 1960. It was particularly interesting to note that the causes of this excess mortality were prominently linked to social and environmental factors. The important point is that this category of causes of morbidity and

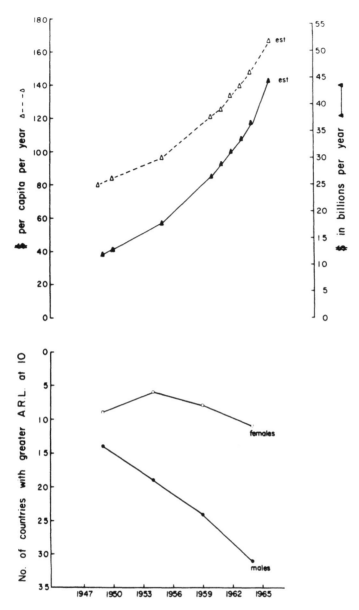

FIGURE 3.1. Total national expenditures for health in the United States and
the per capita expenditures for health, 1949–64, and relative rank in longevity,
United States and other countries. The top curves show the total national
expenditures for health (per billion dollars) in the United States and the per
capita expenditures for health, 1949–64. The bottom curves reflect the relative rank in longevity in the United States in comparison to longevity in
countries that supply data to the United Nations. Longevity is represented by
average remaining lifetime (A.R.L.) after the age of 10 years. est = estimated.
Source: William H. Forbes, "Longevity and Medical Costs," *New England
Journal of Medicine* 227 (1967): 71–78.

mortality lies essentially outside the agenda of traditional clinical medicine. Regardless of how many physicians are trained or how many hospitals are built, what we do to ourselves and to each other will remain little influenced by expenditures made for traditional medical care.

A second explanation refers to the knowledge limitations of medicine. A major success was achieved by science and medicine earlier in the century in dealing with bacterial infectious disease. This success essentially removed these as prominent causes of death. The remaining important contributors to mortality include a very long list of disease processes whose fundamental biological mechanisms and causes are insufficiently understood to permit one to design and institute curative therapy. This category includes a number of chronic degenerative diseases including the diseases collectively known as cancer. Again, investments in traditional clinical medical resources—physicians and hospitals—can be expected to offer very little betterment in the record of mortality from these diseases. Screening, designed to provide for early case finding, has not necessarily led to the promised early or successful (curative) therapy. In fact, as one who carefully examined this question of screening in the United Kingdom, A. L. Cochrane found that early case finding through screening, in many cases, simply lengthened the duration of time between the point at which the disease was recognized and that at which death ensued, without altering the natural course of the disease process.[20]

From the point of view of expenditures made versus health "produced," there has been a second important feature in conjunction with this last point. For a number of reasons (and in the face of the inability to institute definitive or curative therapies), supportive care has taken on a more prominent, more complex, and more expensive role than ever before. Hospitals, for example, have become increasingly filled with technologies—drugs and procedures—that reflect incomplete knowledge and scientific understanding of the diseases to be treated and are designed to support life in a fashion *compensatory* to a disease process rather than *curative* of it. These modes of intervention, which have become known as halfway technologies,[21] are characteristically very expensive, almost always more so than are truly curative or preventive regimens based on adequate scientific understanding. In these terms, the output, health, is necessarily limited by factors that are simply unrelated to the input investments (such as the practice of clinical medicine or the activities within hospital walls).

A third explanation for the apparent disjunction between health and national expenditures for health is that health expenditures have grown rapidly for reasons intrinsic to the health enterprise but in ways in which they could not be expected to "produce" more health. Hospitals, for example, have become both more labor-intensive and more capital-intensive. Capital, used for high-technology items for diagnosis and therapy, has not replaced labor (as in other economic sectors) but has been added to labor. In some instances, new capital inputs have probably *increased* a need for supporting personnel. Further, labor, during the decade of the 1960s, achieved major increases in wage rates from previously very low levels—thereby further increasing their contribution to costs. In an analysis of hospital costs, the economist Martin Feldstein concluded that the "product" provided by hospitals had been dramatically altered principally through an increase in the number of hospital personnel per patient day, higher wage rates, increased use of nonlabor inputs per patient day, and higher prices for nonlabor inputs.[22]

These, then, were the major components of a point of view, which, in 1970, urged a new and careful look at the assumptions of public policy for health of the past. Some of these had been articulated by academic students of the subject for many years. For example, for those who insisted on a long, historical view of health in Western, industrialized nations, the contributions of clinical medicine and medical practice to marked betterment of health status have generally been recognized as overshadowed by other factors, such as nutrition and sanitation.[23] While this situation was recognized by some within the academic and professional fraternities, this was not the kind of heresy that was widely debated among the electorate. Over the next four to eight years, generally because of cost pressures, this general critical line of inquiry into the linkages between national health expenditures and health status would surface in essentially every major industrialized nation. In most cases, the inquiry remained on a fairly academic plane.[24] Nathan Glazer wrote in 1973 in *The Public Interest*: "We are all well aware by now that we should expect little in the way of correlation between health conditions on the one hand and health expenditures, health care facilities use, or system of health care on the other."[25] While one can share Glazer's views about the fundamental issue in this case, one can be much less sure about the extent to which there was general public understanding of or acquiescence in this notion.

Eventually, this issue would be pushed into the arena of public debate. This occurred, perhaps most strikingly, in Canada. In April 1974, the then minister of National Health and Welfare, Marc Lalonde, put before the public a frankly political statement of health and cost of health care in Canada.[26] This "working paper" documented the problems of trying to achieve improvements in health through expenditures made in behalf of traditional forms of medicine and health care. The report, in effect, frankly warned that if the Canadian people truly wished to see improvements in their health status, they were obliged to direct their patterns of health spending in ways that differed markedly from the past. A much milder and much less conclusive statement appeared in the Annual Report of the Council of Economic Advisers in 1972—admittedly not a publication that would generally be considered as common American bedtime reading.[27]

In 1970, this general issue—the disjunction between health status and national expenditures in behalf of health following a prolonged period of marked increase in expenditures—looked to the Office of Science and Technology as if it were appropriate for inclusion in a new and bold statement of public policy. The potential implications looked enormous. On the one hand, presidential espousal of such a concept would seriously question the pattern of health spending which had so marked the prior decade—especially for categorical programs. On the more substantive side, however, and following the reasoning outlined above, a new strategy would direct national attention and funds toward those items of national behavior that were most important in determining health status. Although regulation was the traditional form of the government's response in situations like this, this issue would raise serious questions about the kinds of economic incentives that might be invoked in order to influence the public's smoking and drinking habits, for example.

The strategy implied by this line of reasoning would also put on a firmer basis the biomedical research expenditures made by the federal government. Public monies spent in behalf of biomedical research—mostly through the National Institutes of Health—represented an act of public faith that, ultimately, such spending was in the national interest and would eventually pay dividends in terms of health. Although this matter was not of particular importance while the level of spending was relatively low, it rose in political importance when research expenditures began to compete visibly with other parts of the national budget. In 1970, it seemed clear that, while one could by no means guarantee the productivity of sums spent on biomedical research, one could predict with confidence that the scientific limitations of medicine would continue to contribute increasingly to the disparity between health spending and health. Progress was without question dependent upon the accretion of new scientific understanding.

Finally, it seemed obvious that the control of health care costs—especially hospital costs—would depend on a more thorough understanding of what really contributed to those costs and what were real opportunities for controlling them. In practical terms, the imposing of a new national scheme of health care financing (health insurance) without at first giving suitable attention to an improved organization of the human and institutional elements of the health care system was very liable to provoke in turn a further marked rise in costs.

This point of view was received by the members of the Domestic Council and others on the White House staff with limited zeal. The major problem seemed to be how to translate the central principle into a politically meaningful strategy. Further, the central theme, at first, seemed so markedly foreign to the traditional views that it frightened those whose job it was to deal with political sensitivities. Finally, the implications of following the concept very far towards its logical endpoints carried with them some political liabilities of their own. The best example, of course, would be the official indictment of cigarettes.*

The result was a mixed one. The general framework for a health policy as proposed by the Office of Science and Technology was not adopted. However, discrete elements of it were.

The pattern of categorical government programs—one for each different disease and interest group—was not to be enhanced by further additions. However, this change in policy was made only implicitly—mainly because of the political liabilities associated with threatening existing ties to the federal budget. The surgeon general argued in favor of phasing out the Regional Medical Program. However, his advice was not heeded. A mild nod was given to two specific programs aimed at prevention of ill-health through programs aimed at occupational hazards and alcoholism. The Labor Department's program of occupational safety and health was to be modestly enhanced by a small amount of additional money to assist the establishment of a research arm in HEW to be known as the National Institute of Occupational Safety and Health. In addition, $7 million were to be added to the research program of the National Institute of Drug Abuse and Alcoholism.

A major attempt was made to impose an increase in the Federal excise tax on cigarettes. The options for taxes outlined in the proposal ranged from 2.6 to 5.3 cents per pack—representing an increase in the price of a package of cigarettes of 10 to 20 percent. With assumptions as to how these price increases would affect cigarette consumption, it was estimated that such a policy would raise an additional 0.46 to 0.86 billion dollars annually. The potential uses of these additional revenues included accommodation of farmers dislocated from the growing of tobacco, accommodation of the costs of health care (or those associated with cigarette consumption), or simply augmentation of general revenues. This proposal was included in the option paper sent to the President. However, it did not survive to become a part of the announced health strategy.

---

*All of these were more or less acknowledged some years later, for example, in the Canadian government's stand on health matters.

The proposals and advice given the President concerning research were best described as not highly imaginative. Again, the necessity and cost effectiveness of assuring a scientific basis for clinical medicine were not chosen as explicit principles for policy making. Somewhat in a vacuum of specific proposals, the politically minded machinery of the White House began to make up its own list of targeted projects to highlight. The War on Cancer had already begun. The President had made a commitment to the "War" in his State of the Union Message in January. As both the executive and legislative branches were trying to outbid each other for the public's attention, the President elected to commit an additional $100 million to the National Cancer Plan. As a second research initiative, sickle cell disease was singled out for special attention.

HEW urged that special attention be devoted to research into the factors which contribute to high costs of health care and into organizational and administrative improvements that could be made. This idea had little political appeal and was not adopted, even though it represented a logical step.

Interestingly, a proposal for targeting and directing biomedical research arose from an unexpected quarter. The surgeon general argued strongly in behalf of tighter direction of the elements of the research programs of the National Institutes of Health. One of his specific proposals was for an oversight body (a "Health Research Policy Advisory Committee") to advise on how best to direct or target parts of the research program.*[28]

The Result. Presidential Message on Health to the Congress, 1971

In many ways, the background analysis developed quickly by the Health Policy Review Group was successful. A "decision document" or "option paper" for the President was produced (appendix A). Further, it was developed

---

*The reasoning advanced by the Surgeon General, Dr. Jesse Steinfeld, for this idea is interesting:

Relatively few strictures are placed upon medical researchers, of which there are now approximately 60,000. These scientists are engaged in what is generally referred to as basic biomedical research. This system has worked very well in building a research base unequalled in the world.

However, if the space program had been conducted by NASA on an investigator-initiated project basis, we might well now have 60,000 space scientists, each 80 miles up on the way to the Moon. Where specific goals can be identified, such as the cure of cancer, and where the basic research foundation is adequate, then a research and development technology is necessary, and an additional different kind of research support is needed to produce it.

within three weeks—typical of the kind of heroism that often marks presidential staff work. Most important, it *was* useful and utilized in the real process of directing the government's health affairs for the next several years.

The first step was the insertion of material concerning health into the State of the Union Message. More definitive, however, was the translation of the selected ideas and initiatives into a special presidential message on health to the Congress (appendix B). The preamble of this message ("What's right and what's wrong with American health care") was adopted very directly from the decision paper. Clearly, the major concerns turned around questions of costs and of physical access to care. The question, "what are we getting for all this money?" raised in part because of the science adviser's prodding, was clearly posed in this message. However, the depth of inquiry and the strategies that might have followed from that line of reasoning, were not pursued to their potential endpoints.

Again, most notable was the fact that political judgment considered health of a sufficiently high priority to warrant enunciating a "national health strategy." The principles of equity, efficiency, and prevention, recommended in the background paper, were clearly spelled out in the presidential messages. A fourth one—building on the strengths and preserving the best features of the existing (private) health care system—received a greater emphasis than the background papers had recommended. This clearly was a nod to important constituencies and represented a partisan viewpoint at work. Yet, having offered this conservative viewpoint at the beginning, the message then proceeded to consider the major substantive proposals and initiatives. Of these, the most prominent, health maintenance organizations and national health insurance, were certainly not recognized as the coveted property of the American Medical Association.

Health Maintenance Organization (HMO) was a latter-day name for an older concept—a group practice organization of physicians whose revenues were derived from an agreed upon payment made by their patient-subscribers and received months or a year in advance. The oldest and by far the largest of the prepaid group practices was the Kaiser Permanente Health Care Foundation in California. In 1969, Dr. Paul Ellwood coined the name Health Maintenance Organization and promoted the concept of maintenance of health as opposed to treatment of disease. Whether or not this was a medically sound concept (that is, whether a subscriber cared for by an HMO was more likely to be healthy than one cared for through more traditional medical practice), the scheme had been shown to be financially sound. HMOs' greatest accomplishment was to be seen in their success in keeping patients out of hospitals (where most expenses occurred). Further, the idea looked like a politically sound idea (although it went against the grain of organized medicine). The concept of incentives to "keep people well" was immediately appealing.

The administration had already embraced the notion of HMOs in March 1970 when it proposed amendments to Medicare and Medicaid legislation. HMO was to be offered as an alternative for those classes of patients using the leverage of government funds to promote this concept. Now the government would step out in front of this concept. There would be planning grants and federal loan guarantees for construction to assist the establishment of new HMOs. Further, the federal government would develop a model statute that it was hoped would be adopted by states whose diverse laws, in many cases, limited or inhibited group practice of medicine. Finally, the federal government would make special efforts to encourage the establishment of HMOs in areas particularly marked by a scarcity of health care resources. It is interesting to note as a footnote to this story that the Congress in a clearly partisan fashion delayed any meaningful action on HMOs for the next twenty four months.

A second major initiative was national health insurance. A legislative proposal ("National Health Insurance Standards Act") would oblige employers to provide a minimum program of health insurance for their employees. Employers and employees would share in the cost of this program—depending upon the wage rates of the employees. A lag of ten years was purposely designed to allow for transition, in the hope of pertinent "organizational changes" to accommodate this financing scheme. A second scheme, the Family Health Insurance Plan, was to replace the Medicaid program and was to provide uniform insurance coverage for the poor and for those not employed. The costs of this program would be derived from general federal tax revenues.

The reasoning and the recommendations of the 1969 Carnegie Commission report on medical education were adopted faithfully. The concept of a national scarcity of physicians was accepted and a system of capitation grants to medical schools was adopted. The presidential message even used the Carnegie Commission's own words, "Health Education Centers," when recommending that the education process be distributed more widely and combined with health care service activities.

The message did highlight, to a limited extent, the question of scientific research. However, the initiatives chosen, a further augmented cancer program and the program of investigation into sickle cell disease, were clearly highly selected and targeted—capitalizing on their political appeal as much as their scientific merit.

Epilogue

One of the most striking features of recent American political life is the fact that health, as a national political issue, gradually faded from the scene. There did occur a presidential health message to the Congress in March 1972. However, this message contained essentially no new initiatives.* It did reflect the great extent of partisan "gaming" which, for example, delayed authorizing legislation for national health insurance and for support of the HMO program. Medicaid was not replaced or reformed. The cancer program research budget was increased, as was that for a number of other targeted programs. There were to be some additional initiatives taken in some other fields (such as population and family planning) which were meaningful for health. However, a "comprehensive national strategy for health" as considered at the beginning was not to be realized as such. More important, however, the political rewards that come to a President for taking bold and forward looking initiatives in health began to fade. The "crisis" as the public saw it, was less and less of a real crisis. National health expenditures continued to mount—always ahead of the general rate of inflation—but hidden from public view by existing private and governmental insurance. With the exception of what was clearly an election-related, noontime radio address, there were to be no more presidential messages to the Congress on health for years to come.

---

*Dr. Merlin Du Val, then assistant secretary for health, at the press conference following the message, admitted that there were essentially no changes from the prior year's message.

4. HEALTH-RELATED RESEARCH
AND DEVELOPMENT

In a sense, the matter of how much money the federal government should spend for biomedical research and how those monies should be allocated is a bread and butter issue for a presidential science adviser. It falls into his general charter of helping the government decide on the research and development policies and directions in general. As stated in the beginning of this work, policies for science—matters strictly having to do with R & D—are traditional matters for the Office of the Science Adviser. In general, while they are of vital interest to scientists and engineers, these issues are not always part of the mainstream of political life, which is usually involved with broader, national concerns.

The Annual Governmental Budget Process

The most important channel through which the science adviser deals with R & D expenditures and R & D policies is the budgetary process. Budget making in the federal government occurs through a formalistic ritual which reaches a crescendo in the weeks immediately preceding the President's budget message to the Congress. Those weeks, often termed the "budget season," follow a period of many months of preparations of proposals by the separate agencies and of negotiations between the agencies and the Office of Management and Budget. The period under review in each case is a fiscal year—in real calendar terms, two years removed from the time discussions take place. The budget is influenced by a number of factors including the presidentially agreed on overall level of government spending (a reflection of general economic conditions), continuing commitments from previous years, and the assessment of the merits of each of the various programmatic elements of the long list of governmental activity. In general, the budgeting process has not been an occasion for wholesale review of every program. Rather, it has usually taken the form of marginal or incremental additions to (or subtractions from) the established programs. Interpolated into this relatively systematic scheme as well are the series of "new initiatives." These may be imposed by the President (presidential initiatives) or by congressional directive.

Finally, the executive-congressional interaction is important. The formal process of budget making begins with the President's proposed budget which he sends to the Congress each year in January. Prior to this time, the Congress, through its legislative powers, assigns its spending limits through individual authorizations or budget authorities for each of the many federal programs. Following deliberation and debate over the President's proposals, the Congress imposes its own mark on the budgetary process through this appropriations process. Finally, presidents, from time to time, endeavor to exercise further, usually short-term, control over congressional intentions with regard to appropriations, because of fiscal contingencies or simply political expediency. These last moves are usually limitations on spending through the devices of impoundments or recisions. The complexity of all of this process comes about because these actions are all out of phase, one from another. There are often great uncertainties and delays in reaching appropriation and expenditure decisions. An individual agency not uncommonly is faced with the multiple challenge of working on budgets for three different years at the same time—each one of which is plagued by uncertainties and delays in establishing firm decisions and resolutions.

The Office of Science and Technology articulated with the budgeting process for biomedical research and development through the first half of the 1970s. However, the traditional pattern of influencing R & D patterns and policies through the annual budgetary process became increasingly less satisfactory with time. During the period of major growth of government support for biological and medical research, the Congress (with the help of its constituency of professionals) had offered more money to the NIH each year than the Executive had requested. This pattern began to change in the mid-1960s and the rate of increase in biomedical science appropriations began to decline. Added to this was a growing public reevaluation of the place of science and technology in society. Further, for general economic reasons, during the early 1970s, there were beginning to be limits placed on government spending in general. Large portions of the budget reflected continuing commitments that were difficult to reverse. This left a minority of budgetary items in the "controllable" category—available for short-term political and budgetary influence. Among these were the budgets for research and development. A further factor of importance in the case of biomedical research was the fact that the totality of the government's expenditure had grown to a substantial sum—large enough to be politically visible and competitive with other items in the national accounts. Superimposed on this background came a series of presidential and congressional "initiatives"—programs and new commitments that were put in place as a result of a political response to a desire expressed by some segment of the professional and scientific community. The list of these grew relentlessly through the early 1970s and included cancer, heart and lung disease, family planning, dental caries, environmental health, sickle cell disease, and aging, as well as others. A related question was the extent to which the NIH's research effort should be directed or targeted. The traditional vehicle for funding biomedical research by the NIH had been the research grant for which a single investigator applied in competition with others and which was awarded following the results of a screening process known as peer review. This process of investigator-initiated, peer-reviewed research has long been considered as the most efficient manner of assuring that the scientifically most meritorious ideas and talents were brought into the process of developing lines of research. However, some began to ask whether an element of additional direction should not be added to a portion of the biomedical research activities in order to foster lines of investigation which corresponded to important disease processes but which were less "popular" or fashionable areas of science, to put in place some important applied studies, to assure better coupling between scientific research and the elements of medical care, or to simply accelerate the process of accretion of knowledge.

All of these features conspired during the early 1970s to make orderly planning through the usual budgetary processes difficult. By 1972, the combination of general governmental fiscal stringency (leading to a severe limitation on spending), a much increased level of contract-oriented, targeted research activity, and a growing list of presidential initiatives provoked a series of harsh comments by senior spokesmen for HEW and NIH at the major OMB budget review. In commenting on his view of the "sacred cows" and the lengthy list of presidential commitments, one of them said:

We have had five years of programmatic review for each institute to serve as a guide for allocation. However, the major decisions for re-allocation have been made elsewhere—at a higher level in the Executive Branch, or more often, in the Congress. To an increasing degree, NIH has not had power over a logical allocation.[1]

In the immediate sense, and from the point of view of the traditional scientific establishment, the system was in shambles. From one vantage point that view was a correct one. The old order of things had been shattered and had been replaced by a highly uncertain disorder. Prediction was difficult and stability was no longer assured. Worst of all, the decision process on how much money to spend for medical research and how to spend it seemed to be removed from the exclusive hands of the professionals who now were obliged to share it with those who did political battle generally. The large and visible initiatives such as the National Cancer Program and the augmented National Heart, Lung and Blood Institute, were both praised and fostered by the scientific and professional community as well as condemned by their members. Ambivalence was a common instinct. Morale was low. Out of this anxiety were born a number of exercises designed to influence government thinking, some of which were more appropriate than others. However, this was, in reality, the immediate response to a longer legacy of events. The controversy of the first part of the 1970s (as well as the second part) had origins that really go back to the early history of federal support for medical research.

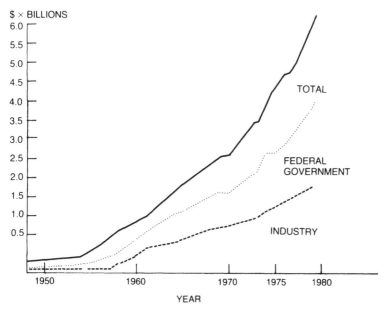

FIGURE 4.1. Total national contribution to medical R & D, 1949–80. Source: U.S., Department of Health, Education, and Welfare, *Basic Data Relating to the National Institutes of Health, 1979*, Washington, D.C., 1979.

History of Federal Investments in Biomedical Research

The National Institutes of Health had been established in 1930 as a successor to the government's Hygienic Laboratory. By 1937, Congress had authorized the National Cancer Institute, and the first research grants were made. The appropriation for research grants for NIH amounted to $85,000 in 1945. Vannevar Bush's postwar scientific review committee recommended that "the amount which can be effectively spent in the first year (1945) should not exceed five million dollars. After a program is underway, perhaps twenty million dollars a year can be spent."[2] By 1950, the level of federal support for medical research had reached $74 million, of which $25 million was attributed to the National Institutes of Health. The total budgetary obligation for fiscal year 1978 for NIH's research and development was $2.58 billion.[3]

The era of major growth began in 1955. The total national expenditures for medical research and development rose from $261 million in 1955 to $4.25 billion in 1974. (Figure 4.1.) The federal share grew from $139 million in 1955 to $2.75 billion in 1974. Of this, roughly 71 percent came from the National Institutes of Health and the National Institute of Mental Health combined.* The industry share of this research grew from $62 million in 1955 to $1.180 billion in 1974. In addition, there has been a small, and in relative terms a declining, contribution from private, nonprofit organizations. In 1974, this contribution amounted to less than 6 percent of the total.[4]

The history of growth of federal support for health research is largely a history of growth of the NIH and the National Institute of Mental Health. (Figure 4.2.) During the two decades following World War II, federal appropriations to NIH and NIMH, largely for biomedical and mental health research, training, and construction activities, increased to $1.224 billion. Between 1957 and 1969, the NIH-NIMH appropriations grew at a compounded annual rate of 24 percent. Yet, after nearly a decade of steady and rapid growth, federal support for health research activities began to level off and, in some instances, decline. These declines were most notable in the share of budgets for research construction and research training. The NIH-NIMH support for the creation of new knowledge through research grants began to decrease in 1967, owing both to the decline in the purchasing power of the dollar and to the increase in the proportion absorbed by indirect or overhead costs of performing research. In a related fashion, the

---

*The Department of Defense and NASA accounted for another 11 percent. The totality from all other agencies amounted to 18 percent.

character of the research enterprise changed over time from one traditionally characterized by individual research projects to one marked by larger and larger teams of researchers and equipment—approaching in some cases the "big science" aggregates of physics.

With this remarkable history, there developed strains and anxieties—generally over matters of funding. On occasion there were insufficient monies. In some instances, it was thought by some that there was perhaps too much. The limits of what constitutes rational or appropriate investment in medical research have never really been clearly discernible.

One fact that does seem clear is that decisions concerning federal support for biomedical research have undeniably become *political* decisions. This is true precisely for the reason that makes other items political in character—success in gaining public financial support in behalf of their endeavor. In this, the community of scientists and physicians had been eminently successful. They had achieved a high level of public spending in their behalf and the rate of rise of these expenditures had been very rapid over a decade and a half. In 1972, Professor Don Price, Dean of the Kennedy School of Public Administration at Harvard, was to observe:

It is important to realize that it was not the lay politicians, but the scientists and professionals, who got medicine into politics, and it is even more important to know how and why. Clearly, they did so by asking the government for a lot of money and you cannot take a lot of tax money without being in politics.[5]

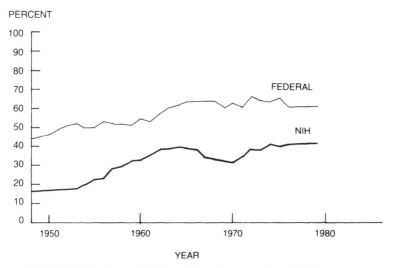

FIGURE 4.2. Federal and NIH contributions to medical R & D as a percentage of total medical R & D, 1950–80. Source: U.S., Department of Health, Education, and Welfare, *Basic Data Relating to the National Institutes of Health, 1979*, Washington, D.C., 1979.

Price's observation is quite correct. Yet, while undoubtedly true, this acknowledgment has not been one made enthusiastically and without reservation by all members of the scientific and professional community. In fact, political visibility, bringing with it features of public accountability and questioning, demands to share decision making more broadly, and inquiries as to results achieved for monies invested are all matters which are perturbing to traditional scientists.

Through the course of this relatively short history, there have been some storm signals raised by members of the scientific fraternity and some outstanding attempts at positive leadership. In 1958, a report of a panel of consultants on medical research to the secretary of HEW (the Bayne-Jones report) clearly indicated anxieties in some quarters over the negative consequences of overly generous public funding of research.[6] These consultants argued the importance of "diversity of Federal and non-Federal sources of support" for biomedical research.[7] They urged that it was "in the national interest for non-Federal support for medical research to be maintained at not less than the (then) current proportions," which was roughly 50 percent of the total.[8] The Bayne-Jones report was remarkably prescient in many ways:

The actual scope of the Nation's medical research effort, the shares of this effort that will be accounted for by private and by public agencies, and the general content of medical research will be determined not only by the economic capacity of the Nation but also by public attitudes and values. . . .[9]

This admonition, fearing unforeseen consequences of unplanned but rapid growth in federal support, was a device to aid in policy choices for later years.

The Consultants find that the past rapid expansion of medical research has met a pressing national need. They are aware, however, of the complex and serious problems imposed thereby. The Consultants point out that the soundest procedure is to increase funds for research on a regular and well-planned basis. . . .[10]

The Bayne-Jones consultants strongly urged the development of an effective mechanism to assist the making of "long-range policy for NIH."[11] In their view, this mechanism should have a strong, perhaps exclusive, contribution from the scientific community itself.[12]

A definitive and comprehensive review of the federal role for biomedical research was completed in 1965 with the publication of the report *Biomedical Science and its Administration*. This review, known as the Wooldridge report, begun in 1963, was in fact managed by the Office of Science and Technology. By 1963, the NIH annual budget was approaching the billion dollar mark. (The Bayne-Jones consultants had estimated that the totality of federal support for biomedical research would not exceed $700 million by 1970.)[13] A major point offered in 1965 by Dr. Dean Wooldridge and his colleagues was the prediction that the NIH would shortly approach "maturity" and, therefore, an extra special effort would be needed to set its priorities and to maintain the "quality of its operation." In particular, the Wooldridge Committee foresaw a period in which the continuously and rapidly rising federal budget for this sector of research would be replaced by a time of relatively level funding. Or, as they expressed it, forthcoming was an "era of relative stability in the fraction of the national effort going into health resources."[14] Because of this leveling off of the federal biomedical research budget, they predicted in turn that there would be, to an increasing extent, competing calls on a scarce resource and, possibly, "inappropriate government control."[15] Because of what they perceived as the importance of these predictions, they offered as their principal recommendation the emplacing of a new instrument to guide and assist in planning and policy decision making. This recommendation for an NIH Policy and Planning Council was never brought into being.

In the years following the Wooldridge report, predictions of budgetary "maturing" did come true. There arose a variety of forces—extrinsic and intrinsic—that tended to influence or even shape the government's major thrust toward the accretion of scientific knowledge for the preventing, treating, and curing of human disease. There did develop competing calls on a scarcer financial resource. It also appears that, in some important ways, the character of research and, hence, the cost of doing biomedical research may have changed, leading to a much higher fraction of the research investment for indirect or supporting costs. Further, many of the ideas specifically dealt with in the Wooldridge report were raised anew—either because the conclusions reached by the former committee were ignored or because new times or new interest groups saw research in a different light. Thus, the targeting of research, the place of investigator-initiated research proposals among other mechanisms for allocating funds for the support of science, the place of peer review, the relationship between the research enterprise (most of it now centered in academic medical centers) and other activities of medical schools, all became questions seeking thoughtful treatment. Uncertainties over predictable budgetary support and over the answers to many of the derivative questions led in the early 1970s to a great deal of uneasiness among members of the biological research community.

The Issues

A major (if not the major) issue is the worth to the nation of public support for medical research. Vannevar Bush, in his famous 1945 report to the President, set apart medical research as an area deserving of special attention. It was Bush's firm belief and that of his Medical Advisory Committee that it was in the nation's best interest that there be public (federal) support for biomedical research in medical schools and universities.[16] Much of the evidence cited referred to wartime successes in dealing with specific disease and injury problems and with public health challenges as part of the war effort. The language used in the report of the Medical Advisory Committee clearly was meant to leave the impression that since the applied medical problems of wartime had been so successfully tackled, adequate public support would just as surely lead the way to the resolution of cancer and arthritis and other prominent contributors to morbidity and mortality.[17]

To some, the extent to which the "production" of health is *science* limited rather than *service* limited is a strong and convincing argument for the public support of biomedical research. To the extent that this "science limitation" is valid and important, one (especially one scientifically trained) is led inescapably to place a value on this effort which is aimed at the creation of new knowledge. Clearly, one of the problems concerns the time constants involved in this research. Investments in biomedical research represent investments with *future* earnings. Payoffs are expected only at some time in the future. Relative to the general public's expectations and common time scales of politically foreseeable events, the length of this "future" is generally quite long.

Thus, on the one hand, the combined medical and scientific fraternity had been particularly successful in persuading the federal government to underwrite the support of medical research. However, as was predicted, the rate of increase in this level of public support began to fall off following a decade and a half. Secondly, because of this very success, the issue of how much money was appropriate for this activity became a political issue—subject to accountability, questioning, and competition from other public desires like all political issues.

Because many were pessimistic about the ability to derive a proper figure through either a rigorous, analytic method of estimate or through consensus of experts, alternate approaches were suggested. One alternative urged that budget levels for biomedical research be sustained so as to bear a constant relationship to some other more basic statistic (GNP, total level of national health expenditures, total national or federal R & D expenditures, etc.). Those who recommended these schemes were as much concerned with the preservation of stability and predictability of the funding levels as they were with finding a rational or systematic scheme for allocating scarce resources.

If there was virtue to the tying of research budgets to some larger, presumably more stable schedule of spending for public and social needs, it was not clear which "anchor" should be chosen nor why. There had not been any dedicated policy of "indexing" or explicitly linking research budgets to other program budgets. Even in the absence of any explicit policy, it is interesting to note that federal R & D and medical R & D budgets have generally borne a more or less consistent relationship to broader national accounts while gaining incrementally and proportionally over a period of several years. (Figure 4.3.) Clearly, to the extent that funds for biomedical research are in competition with other R & D funds, biomedical research has consistently gained in rank since 1956. By 1960, it was 6.2 percent and by 1970, it was 10.2 percent. That is, over a period of fifteen years, medical R & D gained

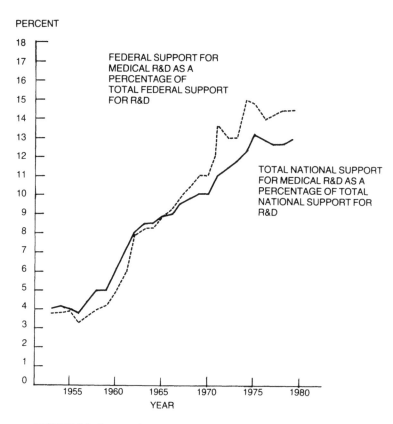

FIGURE 4.3. Support for medical R & D as a percentage of support for total R & D, 1953-80. Source: U.S., Department of Health, Education, and Welfare, *Basic Data Relating to the National Institutes of Health, 1979*, Washington, D.C., 1979; U.S., Office of Management and Budget, *Special Analyses: Budget of the United States Government*, Executive Office of the President, various volumes, 1969 through 1980 fiscal years.

on R & D as a whole at a rate of 0.4 percent per year. Over the same fifteen-year period, the gain of federal spending for R & D was 0.5 percent per year.

As a fraction of the total national expenditures for *health* year by year, the totality of medical research and development rose through the early 1960s and then leveled off and dropped back slightly. (Figure 4.4.) In 1950, medical R & D expenditures represented 1.3 percent of the total national expenditures for health. This rose to 4.5 percent in 1965 and fell back to

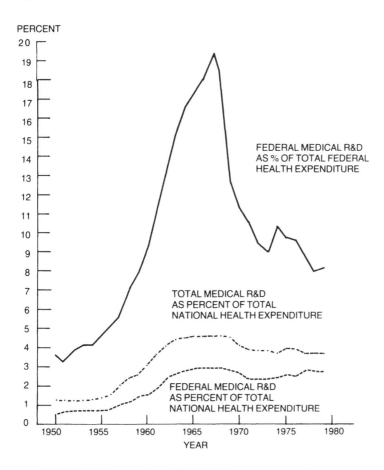

FIGURE 4.4. Support for medical R & D as a percentage of expenditures for health, 1950–80. Source: U.S., Department of Health, Education, and Welfare, *Basic Data Relating to the National Institutes of Health, 1979*, Washington, D.C., 1979; U.S., Social Security Administration, *National Health Expenditures, 1973*, Washington, D.C., 1973; U. S., Department of Health, Education, and Welfare, Health Care Financing Administration, *National Health Expenditures, 1979*, Washington, D.C., 1979.

3.8 percent in 1973. An examination of the Federal expenditures for medical research and development alongside the total of national *health* expenditures reveals a similar relationship (figure 4.4), not unexpected in the face of the relative constancy of the federal contribution to total national biomedical R & D spending. (Figure 4.2.)

The contribution of federal monies for medical research and development relative to total federal health expenditures reveals a different pattern. (Figure 4.4, top graph.) During the 1950s and early 1960s, the fraction of federal health funds dedicated to research rose rapidly—from 3.7 percent in 1950 to 18.1 percent in 1965. This, of course, corresponds in time to the sizable growth in absolute terms of the federal expenditures for biomedical R & D. Beginning just after the middle of the decade of the 1960's, although expenditures for medical R & D continued to rise (figure 4.1), as a percentage of total federal health funds they fell precipitously. In 1966, the percentage was 19.9 percent. In 1967, it had fallen to 12.6 percent. By 1973, it had reached 9.7 percent. The second half of the 1960s, of course, was the period in which new federal responsibilities for underwriting health services (notably Medicare and Medicaid) were born.

There was an additional component in the determination of how much support was appropriate, although it was given less explicit discussion. This philosophy urged the support of science (or particular areas of science) to the extent that the state or capacity of science was ripe with new ideas for exploitation. There is, of course, no rigorous way of determining the "ripeness" of science. Nevertheless, it has generally been assumed that at any point in time, the number of good investigator-initiated grant proposals serves at least as a rough reflection of new scientific avenues available to be followed. The assumption is that the peer review mechanism of filtering these applications refines and orders them on the basis of the quality of the ideas and the worthiness of the proposed projects. The recommendations for approval by the institute advisory councils of NIH were the output of this filtering mechanism. According to this argument, the disparity between the recommendations for approval and recommendations to actually award funds for the approved grants was an index of the failure to take advantage of the capacity of science to push at the frontiers.

The record of reviewing, approving, and awarding for research grant proposals was actually a widely varying one among the NIH institutes when looked at over a ten-year period. (Figure 4.5 and Table 4.1.) There were, in fact, a number of governing variables involved. The number of grants funded was a reflection of both the number of worthy grant proposals and the size of the budget available. If these two factors were held constant (which they were not), a decline in the percentage of funding of approved applications might reflect an increasingly expensive research endeavor due to proportional increases in indirect or overhead expenses or in the changes in the character of research toward intrinsically more expensive units.

With the growth of the National Cancer Program beginning in 1971, it became common to attempt comparisons and contrasts between the experience of the National Cancer Institute and that of the remainder of the NIH institutes. (Figures 4.6 and 4.7.) The NCI award record was a more favorable one in these terms than the average record for NIH—probably reflective of a complex of factors including the deliberate attempt intrinsic to the cancer program to "saturate" the field and to accommodate to the maximum extent the existing fund of scientific ideas.[18] There may also be a shift in the direction of grant proposals toward the augmented cancer monies. (Note that none of these analyses speaks to the quality of the research ideas and proposals, which was not necessarily uniform over time or among subject areas.)

There were several other important issues of science and public policy which were derivative of the central question, how much money was enough

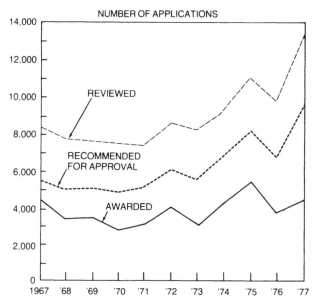

FIGURE 4.5. NIH competing research grant applications reviewed, recommended for approval, and awarded, fiscal years 1967-77. (Includes NIEHS and NLM, and excludes NIMH and BHME for all years. Includes amended applications; excludes applications with budget periods of 24 months or more.)
Source: U.S., Department of Health, Education, and Welfare, *Basic Data Relating to the National Institutes of Health, 1979*, Washington, D.C., 1979.

TABLE 4.1

Council Approved Grants and Award Rates for NIH Competing Research Grants

Fiscal Years 1969, 1971, 1973, 1974, 1977

NIH Component	Number of Grant Applications Reviewed by Councils					Percentage Recommended by Council for Funding					Percentage of Council Recommendations Awarded				
	1969	1971	1973	1974	1977	1969	1971	1973	1974	1977	1969	1971	1973	1974	1977
National Institute on Aging	....	....	....	....	330	....	....	....	....	63.3%	....	....	....	....	64.6%
National Institute on Allergy and Infectious Disease	920	838	965	1000	1053	66.5	75.1	70.7	83.3	80.4	57.8	45.8	37.6	49.7	33.6
National Institute on Arthritis and Metabolic Diseases	1623	1318	1310	1409	1754	69.7	72.5	77.9	80.8	77.3	65.5	46.4	34.3	63.3	53.7
National Cancer Institute	829	922	1736	1939	2894	63.7	68.1	63.9	70.0	64.9	55.9	68.2	59.6	71.1	47.2
National Institute of Dental Research	245	265	266	261	388	57.6	52.8	58.6	52.1	55.7	52.5	62.9	47.4	65.7	57.2
National Institute of Environmental Health Sciences	103	133	188	218	252	50.5	63.9	62.2	72.0	77.8	59.6	60.0	38.5	60.6	61.7
National Eye Institute	....	226	380	360	468	....	79.6	81.1	85.0	83.5	....	65.6	40.3	51.8	64.1
National Institute of General Medical Sciences	1100	1127	1365	1173	1493	71.2	79.6	78.2	82.8	83.1	56.8	36.1	31.9	51.1	38.7
National Institute of Child Health and Human Development	918	1032	1302	1324	1179	54.8	58.1	61.4	67.0	65.1	50.1	39.7	33.6	45.4	42.6
National Heart, Lung and Blood Institute	1082	1172	1382	1559	2101	60.0	65.0	70.1	66.5	71.6	78.4	62.1	46.7	63.0	55.0
National Institute of Neurological, Communicative Disorders and Stroke	1080	945	1120	1181	1088	68.1	61.8	69.0	76.5	68.1	87.1	59.8	35.1	59.1	39.0
Division of Research Resources	129	102	221	191	175	71.3	69.6	71.0	75.9	76.0	71.7	70.4	43.3	89.0	77.9
Total	8029	8080	10225	10615	13175	65.1	68.5	70.7	74.0	71.9	65.2	51.5	40.7	61.9	48.0

Source: U. S., Department of Health, Education and Welfare, Basic Data Relating to the National Institutes of Health, Washington, D. C., v.1974; v. 1975; and v. 1978.

to assure the adequate public support of biomedical science. One of these derivative or second-order issues was how best to set priorities and how to allocate wisely the research funds among various broad categories of research. This subject was elevated to the level of heated discussion when the balance between budgets for cancer research and those for other categories of investigation were altered.[19] A related question was whether and how to exercise direction of research within generic research categories. This question was often paraphrased by the choices, to target or not to target.

Both notions were subtended by the concept of setting priorities among the broad menu of research choices. The Wooldridge review had been quite explicit:

NIH devotes its principal effort to a broad program of prevention of specific diseases. It employs this approach for a single and valid reason: life science is so complex, and what is known about fundamental biological processes so little, that the "head-on" attack is today frequently the slowest and most expensive path to the cure and prevention of disease.[20]

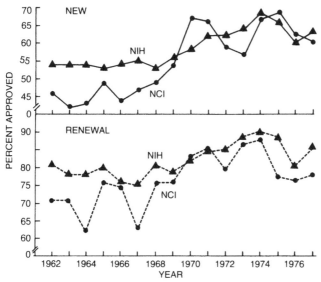

*PERCENT OF NUMBER REVIEWED

FIGURE 4.6. Approval rates, as a percentage of number reviewed, for traditional grants, National Cancer Institute versus all of NIH, 1962–76. Source: John T. Kalberer, Jr., and Thomas J. King, *Report on Grant-Supported Research Programs*, Report presented to the National Cancer Advisory Board (Washington, D.C.: U.S., Department of Health, Education, and Welfare, Division of Cancer Research Resources and Centers, May 1978).

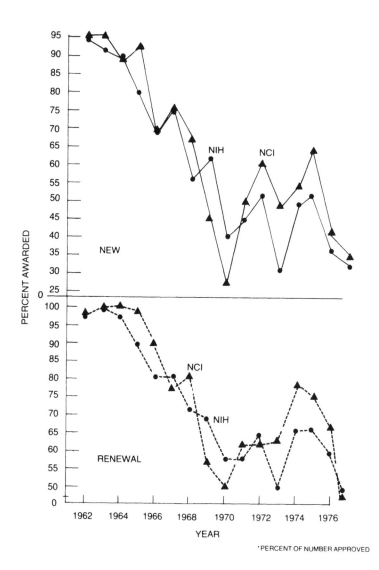

FIGURE 4.7. Award rates, as a percentage of number approved, for traditional grants, National Cancer Institute versus all of NIH, 1962–76. Source: John T. Kalberer, Jr. and Thomas J. King, *Report on Grant-Supported Research Programs*, Report presented to the National Cancer Advisory Board (Washington, D.C.: U.S., Department of Health, Education, and Welfare, Division of Cancer Research Resources and Centers, May 1978).

Yet, no more than a year had passed after the publication of the Wooldridge report when a second advisory committee headed by Jack Ruina felt compelled to note that "the most significant change in the nature of NIH support of biomedical research has been the emergence in recent years of programs of directed research or development."[21]

Support of research according to categories of disease had become a long-established phenomenon. It was early recognized that the electorate and its elected Congress could best identify with specific disease problems. Cancer was selected first and there followed in succession a series of nine more NIH institutes, each bearing identification with a serious recognized disease process or with an organ system that stood for a category of diseases. Names of the institutes, as with voluntary health organizations, were early recognized to be important[22] and the "which Senator or Congressman ever died of microbiology" syndrome caused many to think carefully about this subject of identification.[23] (It is hardly surprising that the one institute bearing the most nonspecific title, General Medical Sciences, was the one most affected in time of budgetary constraint.) The result was something of a compromise— just enough categories to assure financial backing, yet no more than are necessary in order to preserve the best of the undifferentiated and seren- dipitous character of scientific endeavor. In recent years, however, there had been pressures—at times severe—from both scientists and lay spokesmen to add to the list of categorical institutes of the NIH family. Aging, population and family planning, diabetes and gastrointestinal diseases, all joined a list from time to time as candidates for new, independent NIH institutes.

An essential ingredient in making this compromise workable in practice had been the ingenious balance achieved through the effective use of NIH study sections and councils for setting priorities and for making individual research project decisions (peer review). Traditional scientists argued forcibly that direction or management of lines of investigation and choices of ex- periments should be governed by the professional views of those within the field—through investigator initiated research with peer review. Such a system was at the same time the best and the worst of all worlds. It clearly was the best known method of arriving at choices among scientific details. It used the judgment of those most knowledgeable of the field and the best equipped to appreciate the appropriate scientific opportunities of the area. Peer review, in addition, was an effective and efficient mechanism for getting a critical judgment from among several expert parties. The flaw, of course, was that since peer review was, by definition, scientists contemplating the ideas of other fellow scientists, the public needed reassurance from time to time that such a system, living as it did from public revenues and done in the public's behalf but out of view of the public, was science for its social sake as well as science for science's sake—an investment activity as well as a consumption activity.[24]

The Ruina report, of course, was commissioned in 1966 to deal precisely with this subject.[25] A ground rule or basic assumption of that study was that direction of both research and development was desirable and inevitable. A principal finding of the report was the necessity of developing a new, "strong management structure" to accommodate and foster the direction of research and development within NIH.[26]

There seemed to be several concerns raised in the debates over the issue of how best to direct and manage research. One was the fundamental fear that direction, per se, was unwise, unproductive, or unworkable. A second was anxiety over the diffusion of the research effort to organizations other than traditional academic medical centers and nonprofit research institutes. A third was, perhaps, a fear of partial emasculation of the traditional advisory committee mechanisms that have characteristically (and by statute) held a powerful influence over research programs and choices.

The debates were by no means settled,[27] and were clearly heightened by the advent of the augmented National Cancer Programs and by the terms of the National Heart, Lung, and Blood Program. An outstanding feature of the cancer program was an explicit statement of need for a mechanism to administer a "coherent program" and a call for a "comprehensive national plan"[28] —in one respect, a large-scale experiment on how best to do research —by targeting or by not targeting.

A second derivative issue concerned where this research effort should best be carried out. The original concept in the creation of the National Institutes of Health was of a strong (if not exclusive) intramural research organization—related in character perhaps, to the U.S. Geological Survey. That concept of preference for strong intramural programs began to weaken in 1937 with the creation of the National Cancer Institute.[29]

It was clear that Vannevar Bush and his Subcommittee on Medical Research[30] looked mainly to universities as the principal focus for medical research and viewed the NIH at least as much as a broker of research funds as it was a doer of research. Although there were striking differences among the patterns of the various institutes, this general trend of supporting research in university medical centers became increasingly marked with the passage of time. The growth of the 1950s and the 1960s was largely growth in extramural, grant-supported activities in universities.

In 1947, more than 60 percent of the federally supported investigations in the life sciences were performed in government laboratories and about 25 percent went toward the support of science departments of institutions of higher education. Between 1947 and 1966, intramural research activities grew at a rate of 17 percent per year while extramural support increased at an average rate of 27 percent. By 1966, 75 percent of the total federal expenditure for biomedical research was dedicated to extramural support. Two-thirds of this went to educational institutions—most of which were medical schools or were universities that contained medical schools.[31] The Wooldridge report urged a furtherance of this pattern, relying heavily on the arguments that universities were the repositories of the best scientific talent and that research and education were inextricable.[32] With the advent of the National Cancer Program came even further exaggeration of the trend of placing NIH in a broker position—mainly because of the sizable task involved in servicing and overseeing contractual arrangements.

The Carnegie Commission on Higher Education in 1970 hinted broadly that the traditional joint venture arrangement might not be so inviolate as it had sometimes been thought.[33] The pragmatic argument had been, as always, money. The instabilities of research funding seemed to weigh heavily against the advantages of developing interlocking dependencies between medical education and medical research and, to some, seemed a forceful argument against ever again allowing these dependencies to develop.[34]

A related issue was the question of whether research choices should be selected primarily for quality or should also aim toward the development of capacity. In 1965, the twenty five educational institutions receiving the largest sums from federal sources for medical research performed 50 percent of all of the federally financed medical research done at institutions of higher education—amounting to $267 million.[35] The relative virtues of building on the best of the quality of the national research enterprise versus the more egalitarian development of the total research potential was earlier highlighted by the short-lived Centers of Excellence Program.

An important and clearly unresolved issue, thoroughly intertwined with the issues of research per se, was that of manpower needed to perform research. This was a thoroughly confused subject for several reasons, and badly needed to be studied and clarified. First of all, there was the core question of how many of what types of trained manpower were needed or desired. (The answer to this question, of course, depended heavily on the particular research policy chosen—whether for maximum quality, maximum accommodation to the scientific opportunities at any point in time, or other.) Second was the particular question of a federal government's role in influencing scientific manpower supplies. Much of the traditional analysis had been concerned with attempts to match numbers of persons needed to expected supplies. These analyses, inevitably difficult, are subject to a variety of assumptions. Estimates of both supply and demand are arrived at with difficulty and, in many cases, have been reflections of specific needs in universities rather than large societal needs.[36] The matter was greatly complicated because of the long time often required for research to show productive results. A decision to prime the pump of training, typically reflective of an immediate snapshot of manpower needs, cannot produce productive researchers for many years, during which both national and scientific priorities may change sharply. Thus, national programs and policies have been characterized by hysteresis for years.

Numbers aside, the National Institutes of Health (and others) viewed the federal role in the training of medical research manpower as primarily one of maintaining quality, not quantity.[37] This was a major argument behind the dual vehicles of funding in this area—stipends for trainees and support for the institutions that provided the training settings. There was again the nagging problem of dependency of medical schools on the federal government that developed as a result of past policies and programs—making reviews and revisions of past decisions particularly difficult, rational arguments notwithstanding.[38]

Role of the Office of the Science Adviser

Traditionally, the director of the Office of Science and Technology (who was, as well, the President's science adviser) was chosen from among accomplished physical scientists. The rationale, in part, included the fact that it was in behalf of the physical sciences and engineering that the federal government devoted the largest portion of its research and development funds. However, it had become somewhat traditional in later years as well to appoint as deputy director someone drawn from the fraternity of biological and medical sciences—in part to emphasize the importance with which the Science Adviser viewed the biological sciences. This pattern began essentially with the new organization of the science adviser's function in 1962. Except for a hiatus of several months in 1969 when there was no representative of the medical sciences, medicine and biology were included among the portfolio of disciplines in the White House office.

In late 1969, to the fraternity of research scientists in medicine and biology, the instabilities of funding appeared ominous. Federal budgets for training of researchers and for construction of research facilities had been severely cut back. Those for research itself seemed to be in jeopardy because of a number of forces. Research programs carefully developed and nurtured over the years in medical schools and teaching hospitals—indeed in response to earlier federal incentives and signs of encouragement—were subject to an uncertain future. The linkages between medical research and medical education, which had become so secure as to be taken for granted, were subject to new scrutiny. Those linkages, which had developed a kind of sacred quality extending back to the time of Abraham Flexner, were suddenly questioned by even another part of the establishment with the publication of the Carnegie Commission report in 1970.[39]

Uncertainties were felt in a most pronounced fashion in medical schools and academic medical centers. The signals from the federal establishment were unclear, marked by discontinuities and seeming contradictions. For example, there were ever present pressures to increase the number of professional resources available to practice medicine. Yet, the kind and the quality of the medicine these practitioners were to provide were less clear. The academic medical community had devoted an extraordinary effort extending over a period of half a century to assuring the scientific basis of medicine and of medical training. As a part of this effort, the United States had indeed led the world in essentially all areas of biomedical research. The continuation of that legacy now seemed in doubt. Public confidence in things scientific and technical was beginning to ebb. The compartmentalization of medicine into narrow (if exceedingly capable) subspecialties was increasingly questioned. Some even chose to blame the high scientific content of medicine for its rapidly rising cost. In brief, the public display of critical questions about health, and about health care and its practitioners, carried with it a wide pattern of fallout, some of which was visited upon medical research and its traditional ties to medical education.

The Office of Management and Budget questioned the wisdom of continued training of medical researchers. There developed a general dissatisfaction with the federal subsidization of any type of professional training. In medicine, however, the argument against training seemed particularly strong since the income of practicing physicians was clearly high and it was reasoned that M.D.'s who chose a career of research could afford to support their own training. The federal budget bureaucracy even questioned further increases in money to support research itself, suggesting that such programs would simply create augmented demand for persons to be trained—perhaps at public expense as well.

To some, there appeared to be a compelling need to set the record straight where the public's and the government's thinking was muddled. The Wooldridge report had been a good and thorough review of a wide variety of important issues. It had seemed to bring an element of reassurance and stability at the time. However, public and governmental attitudes change remarkably quickly and 1965 (the date of issuance of the Wooldridge document) seemed to be a long time back.

Accordingly, it was proposed that the President's Science Advisory Committee would adopt as one of its important tasks the review of certain important issues concerning biomedical research and the relationship between medical research and health care. More accurately, the President's Science Advisory Committee took upon itself the accomplishment of this review. The self-generated nature of this inquiry was important in determining the way its product was ultimately received by the political machinery. The committee members felt it incumbent upon themselves to exercise responsible leadership for this area—to step out in front of this important set of issues. It seemed only logical that the force of a persuasively done review from an authoritative body would set the record straight and help policymakers steer a correct course. There were at least two flaws in this scheme, however. There was no patron within the political machinery who felt he wanted the advice. None had requested it. To proffer it smacked strongly of academic scientists' advocating more and continued federal largesse for themselves. Further, and in a related fashion, its very subject did not fit well into any of the important contemporary political frameworks. It seemed out of step with the series of important public questions concerning health and health care. The old coalitions in the legislature that had, for years, supported the NIH budgets were no longer prominent. Government fiscal responsibility was an important, if perhaps short-range, necessity. In brief, this offering was ultimately to become not very useful to the political decision processes.

A PSAC Panel on Biological and Medical Science was organized in late 1969. The terms of reference or charter for this panel were interesting. (See appendix C for a text of those terms of reference.) The focus for this study was clearly on biomedical research. However, there was a kind of omnibus list of other features relating to health care and medical education designed to characterize the linkages between research and service and to demonstrate their importance to the politically prominent aspects of health care. For example, the text of this document noted that there was "a growing lack of coordination, approaching confusion, among *national goals* in therapeutic and preventive medicine, delivery of health care, improvement of environmental quality, mental health, nutrition, etc., the quality of *programs* to achieve them, and the *resources* allocated to this purpose."[40]

The PSAC Panel on Biological and Medical Science, under the chairmanship of Dr. Ivan Bennett, worked through late 1969 and all of 1970 on a report directed to the President. Early drafts made modest attempts to refer to health needs of the nation.[41] However, the document remained strongly focused on issues of research and of the training of researchers. It spoke to the necessity of making investments in new knowledge in order to treat with the important diseases whose fundamental causes were essentially unknown. It discussed the expensive implications of compensatory or "half-way" technological interventions in therapy that medicine invoked when practitioners were unable to deal definitively with diseases. It treated with what the panel considered to be the carefully developed and highly effective linkages between medical research and medical education.

Hence, the report was fundamentally concerned with research, with researchers, and with those institutions where most of the research was performed, namely, universities. The panel expressed concern for drug addiction and alcoholism and for the challenge of mental illness. The recommendation in this case was for research into the "medical-social" causes of ill-health. There was a call for special attention to research into how health care systems worked and didn't work. Targeted or directed areas of research were sanctioned, but for delimited segments of science and only through the appropriation of new funds, so as not to compete with the traditional core programs. Finally, it was strongly urged that training of biomedical research manpower be supported by the federal government.

In a number of interesting aspects, the panel took issue with elements of common wisdom of the day and with findings of other expert groups. The need for 50,000 additional physicians, which had become the accepted litany and which had been amplified by the Carnegie Commission's report, was clearly questioned by the PSAC panel. Their recommendation was that the output of existing medical schools should be increased by 25 percent over a five-year period. They urged that a number of creative methods be found to assist the funding of medical education—federal incentive payments to medical schools, student loan programs and an "Educational Opportunity Bank." The panel questioned the desirability of fostering large numbers of general practitioners and it discouraged any suggestion of government direction or influence over what kind of medicine a physician practiced or where he practiced it.

Finally, the panel recommended that the evolution of a national health policy was worthy of special attention. For this, they urged the establishment within the Executive Office of the President of a group dedicated to the formulation of national health policy and to the preparation of an annual report on national health goals and programs.

To suggest that the panel's work was not well received would be to understate the facts. The President was persuaded to meet with the panel in

September 1970. However, the panel's findings were simply not useful to public policy makers. Their report treated only modestly or not at all with what were publicly perceived major problem areas in health. Further, in some instances, the panel had challenged other established views, such as the need for general practitioners or the need for more practitioners. These translated into meaningful political action. Additional research was not a very satisfying solution for what others described as pressing public problems. There were indeed recommendations for government expenditure, but for the most part these tended to confirm further what many politicians feared from this quarter—advocacy by members of the academic community for more public funds for the pursuit of science in academic settings.

The final report was never issued. Even though a signed presidential statement was prepared and copies were printed, the release of the report was not permitted.[42] Most important, internally the findings of this panel had scarcely any influence on the real processes of political thinking and formulation of the "National Strategy for Health" that was proceeding at roughly the same time.

Two other attempts were made to bring the advice of the President's Science Advisory Committee on related health issues to bear on the political machinery during this period. One was a further study of the needs for training of scientific researchers;[43] the other was a study of the importance of research on the organization and administration of health care itself.[44]

The government continued to question the wisdom of further federal support for the training of biomedical research scientists. The administration had assumed a posture against government subsidization of training in general. This was further reinforced by an overlay of limiting government spending generally. For a brief period in the early 1970s, a traditional shortage of scientists turned into an oversupply creating public stories of underemployment of scientists.

A study panel of the President's Science Advisory Committee was assembled to examine the question of how necessary or worthwhile was the continuation of a government program of support for training of scientists and in what forms should the support best be provided. The findings of this panel were in favor of support. The arguments were eminently logical and reasonably far seeing. Research was the foundation of any progress in medicine. The pipeline of discovery and of new ideas had to be kept filled in order to assure useful innovations later on. This, in turn, meant that bright and imaginative young researchers had to be brought into the fraternity of science continuously. Simple market forces as incentives (the proposal of some within the government structure) would not be sufficient to induce sufficient good talent into research.

Again, this work was proffered, not solicited. The target was the Office of Management and Budget. Its spokesmen listened to the findings of the panel and to members of the panel. However, they remained unmoved in their more doctrinaire positions. To OMB, these were still academic scientists seeking ways to augment their share of federal largesse. Why should biomedical research training be treated any differently from other forms of professional training, they asked. Further, what could possibly be politically less popular than the subsidization of a fraternity whose practitioners already claimed some of the highest levels of personal income?

The PSAC Panel on Health Services Research and Development concerned itself with an area of medical investigation which departed sharply from the traditional line of endeavor identified with the National Institutes of Health. In 1967, a new institution, a National Center for Health Services Research and Development, was created within the Department of Health, Education, and Welfare to foster research into ways of improving the organization and management of health care systems. The purpose of the center was to engage talent of a variety of disciplines in university settings in behalf of finding administrative and organizational improvements in health care. As a result, it was hoped, the nation might realize a betterment in the quality, or reduction in the costliness, of medical care. The center had been only a modest success. It had been placed administratively well down in the bureaucracy of HEW. Its own early leadership had been weak. Most of all, perhaps, there was little constituency in behalf of what it was supposed to do. The traditional fraternity of medical practitioners had little interest in either its goals or its methods. Its preoccupations seemed more allied to matters of economics or management than to medicine. Its activities bore little relationship to the traditional types of research associated with NIH, and its monies were not hotly sought after by aspiring scientific minds in university settings. Further, its very name did not incite the enthusiasm of Congressmen who more easily identified with categorical diseases such as cancer and arthritis.

Yet the need for finding ways of improving the nation's health care system through systematic study and through the application of scientific method seemed eminently logical. The PSAC panel was designed to take stock of progress in this field and to recommend an appropriate federal role.

The resulting report of the panel, headed by Dr. Kerr White, was particularly thorough. It surveyed the results to date. It considered the sum of potential contributions of health care research to improvements in health care. It related all of these to identifiable problems of cost and availability of services. It recommended that there was indeed an appropriate governmental role for this area of research. It also urged that health policy making within the federal government be more structured and more systematic.

The panel's work was not particularly influential in government thinking. The report was publicly released, but only on a limited basis.[45] No new initiatives followed from it. Further, the budget of the existing National Center for Health Services Research and Development continued to fall to approximately a third of what it had once been.

Epilogue

The most fundamental issues considered were the appropriate size of the federal expenditures for biomedical research and its proper or best allocation among specific areas of research. The federal government—NIH, in particular—did not heed the advice of the Wooldridge Committee which urged that scientists and NIH assume a lead role in directing that process, systematically and rationally. Thus, as budgets became increasingly more stringent, predictions of unhappiness within the scientific community came true.

The position taken by the panels of the President's Science Advisory Committee were clearly not helpful in articulating with the political process of that era. In my view, they would not have been useful in any recent era. Influence in the budget negotiations each year was moderate but not extraordinary. OST's strong identification with those scientists who argued for federal subsidies for professional training probably succeeded in losing intragovernmental support for the science adviser's office as an objective, third-party opinion.

The meaningful debates were waged in other forums, at other levels, and on different issues. The details of the President's National Health Strategy were developed quickly—and by a totally dedicated body of people (as described in the previous chapter). The science adviser's office was a part of that process and was represented by this author. The opportunity to influence the policy thinking at that point was sizable—especially for certain short-term issues and only if spokesmen carefully guarded their positions of objectivity and nonadvocacy. Another example was the debate over the details of the much augmented National Cancer Plan. Here, the science adviser's role in brief was principally that of preventing massive administrative rearrangements and potentially destructive personnel changes which were advocated by some within the political inner circle.

The fundamental issues in biomedical research did not vanish but, in fact, became even more prominent in time. Daniel Greenberg wrote in the *New England Journal of Medicine* in 1974 that the setting of priorities for medical research was something that deserved serious attention.[46] He hinted that if the members of the biomedical community did not take a strong leadership role in cooperation with other spokesmen, the political process would perform the task without the assistance of professionals. Following his tenure as assistant secretary for health, Dr. Charles Edwards spoke in the same year of the essential dilemma facing the scientific community as one of conflict between freedom and accountability:

There is no easy escape from this dilemma. Clearly, science cannot accede entirely to public pressure; to do that would be to reject the freedom of inquiry that is essential to fundamental research. But by the same token, science cannot remain aloof from society. It cannot pursue its own ends in complete disregard for the will and expectations of the people whose support it needs. . . .

What I am suggesting is that scientists very much need to take the initiative in the determination of science policy and the selection of scientific priorities.[47]

The 1970s did see the growth of ferment and uneasiness within the biomedical research community. The legacy of past programs and government policies that encouraged research programs led to the dependence of universities and medical schools on biomedical research and research training funds. In many cases, the research monies became inextricably interwoven with those supporting other activities in medical school settings. Budgetary uncertainties tended to make the academic community very anxious indeed (although that community was not suitably galvanized to assist thoughtful public discussion). Professional societies in many cases organized "public affairs" groups designed to inform their membership and to educate their Congressmen.[48] In a few instances, book-length public reports emerged that proclaimed the public benefit of investment in a strong research program for biomedical sciences.[49]

In October 1973, Senator Abraham Ribicoff, partly as a result of the prodding of former HEW Secretary Wilbur Cohen, brought together over lunch a group of "alumni" of NIH. Senator Ribicoff sought the professional judgments of this group preliminary to holding a series of intended hearings on this subject. Principally because he did not possess jurisdiction in this area, the Ribicoff hearings were not held.

With time, additional urgency was added to this issue. The National Institutes of Health and its directors were pressed by a number of parties to the issue. Spokesmen for the scientific community publicly expressed anxieties—generated, presumably, partly from insecurities over their funding, partly from true convictions over the perceived status of medical research, and most of all because of uncertainty concerning national priorities. Advisers to NIH expressed their views—sometimes forcibly, as occurred during one of the meetings of the National Heart and Lung Institute's Advisory Council in March 1974.

Finally, Congress, in reflecting these concerns as well as other motivations, was pressed to consider a vehicle for "settling the issue." One version of the proposed amendments to the 1974 extension of the National Cancer Plan called for the establishment of a three-man President's Biomedical Research Panel modelled in part on the National Cancer Panel. This particular proposal was traded in the Conference Committee for a more orthodox Biomedical Research Panel.[50] This was the origin of the President's Biomedical Research Panel which, once again, was charged with assessing the state of biomedical and behavioral research.[51]

The President's Biomedical Research Panel, whose chairman was Dr. Franklyn Murphy, generated a great deal of highly useful testimony and background studies. Its scope of exploration was suitably broad and deep. However, the report and findings of the panel itself were strikingly constrained. The panel stepped back from more issues than it addressed. Accordingly, fundamental challenges remain unsettled. The even less well organized attempt by HEW Secretary Califano two years later at developing a "comprehensive five-year research plan" and at developing "research planning principles"[52] is, again, symptomatic of the lack of suitable resolution of some basic questions about how much public tax money should be dedicated to biomedical science and how this money should be allocated among the several areas of research.

5. THE ENVIRONMENT, HEALTH, AND REGULATION TO PROTECT HEALTH

Historical Background

The federal government has had a fairly long history of concern for the integrity of the physical and chemical environment. The traditional form of this concern was the provision of data, support of research and surveys, education, and guidelines for state and regionally administered programs to deal with air and water pollution. The Department of the Interior had major responsibilities for air and water pollution. For those pesticides used on agricultural products destined to become foodstuffs, the Food and Drug Administration shared with Agriculture certain responsibilities for monitoring, research, and regulation. There were in addition major areas of concern by the FDA for the quality and character of foodstuffs, for the efficacy and safety of therapeutic drugs, and to a lesser extent, for the safety of cosmetic products. Principal responsibilities for scientific studies and regulatory actions aimed at protection from ionizing radiation fell to the Atomic Energy Commission.

That brief description betrays a neatly compartmentalized structure of government. In fact, the overlaps and fragmentation were considerable. Jurisdictional responsibilities, resulting from authorizing legislation plus numerous later amendments, were widely spread and comprised a very complex labyrinth. Furthermore, repeated governmental reorganizations over the years had often succeeded in moving administrative boxes to new locations so frequently that a given governmental agency not uncommonly found it difficult to truly accomplish its substantive mandate.

It is possible to offer a few basic generalizations concerning the government's role in environmental and regulatory matters.

1. Regulation has traditionally been the chosen governmental vehicle for dealing with matters of the environment. Other alternatives, such as education or economic incentives, have generally been rejected or given only nominal attention.

2. Through the years, there evolved an increasingly rich fabric of regulatory laws. New, more elaborate and more stringent regulatory devices were laid on typically on the occasion of a public "crisis"—an event in which a new or unchecked threat to health was revealed. The Food and Drug Administration was granted new authorities after the elixir of sulfanilamide crisis of 1938 and again following the Thalidomide disaster in 1962.

3. The nominal basis for much of the regulatory activity aimed at preservation of the integrity of the physical environment has been the protection of human health. Health was often a surrogate for other desirable features of the physical environment because, typically, health was a more salable item politically.

4. Alongside the historical trend of increasing elaboration of the tools of regulation has been a second and complementary trend. This has been the separation of the regulatory and protection functions of government from the promotional ones. Successively, the nation through its Congress had demanded that an institutional distinction be made between those agencies of the government responsible for encouraging the productivity in agriculture or favoring the development of new drugs and those responsible for protection from those products or by-products. The Food and Drug Administration, which began its life as a part of the Department of Agriculture, was separated from it and made a part of the Federal Security Agency in 1940, and of the Department of Health, Education, and Welfare in 1953. Similarly, the Nuclear Regulatory Commission was set apart from what had formerly been the combined promotion and protection functions in the Atomic Energy Commission.

5. In addition to the regulatory parts of the federal establishment, the government has underwritten a sizable effort at research aimed at understanding the environmental contribution to human disease. The two major elements are the National Cancer Institute of NIH and the program of research into the biological effects of ionizing radiation, for years supported by AEC and, more recently, by the Department of Energy. However, there are programs of research dealing with man's environment and his health in other parts of the government, including other parts of NIH, the National Institute of Occupational Safety and Health, and the Environmental Protection Agency.

The end of the 1960s saw a ground swell of public interest in matters of the environment. The combination of years of industrial development and exploitation of natural resources, growth of the population and of its mobility, raised serious national concerns for the future of man's environment. Scientific knowledge had contributed to these anxieties by increasing the sensitivity and resolution of the methods of measurement and monitoring— leading to the identification of increasingly small traces of environmental contaminants. Science had contributed, too, by raising new scientific hypotheses and by scientific experiments aimed at elucidating what problems human and industrial activity might visit upon the health of people exposed to environmental agents.[1] Finally, one should add the importance of sufficiency of national and personal wealth and of disposable income which permitted the nation the luxury of turning its attention toward environmental concerns.

The new administration came into office in 1969 as the tide of national concern for environmental quality was still rising. As a political issue, the country seemed unequivocally behind it. Local bond issues for environmental improvement passed handily. Much attention was given to environmental matters by the press. The Congress responded by producing a wealth of legislative proposals for budgeting expenditures, for administrative reorganization, and for further regulation.

The Pre-Inaugural Task Force on Resources and Environment, whose chairman was Russell Train, took note of the political popularity of this issue. The task force recommended giving appropriate visibility to environmental matters and matching expectations of fulfillment of financial commitments for government programs to the promises made during the course of campaigning for office. It recommended a serious attempt to make the existing government programs more effective but urged no "mammoth new programs."[2]

Earlier Involvement of the President's Science
Adviser in Environmental and Related Health Issues

The science advisory mechanism had touched on matters of the environment and health at times during its history. From 1959 onward, the Office of Science and Technology (and its antecedent organization) was increasingly involved with the character of the physical environment and with factors which affected the environment. In 1959, the secretary of Health, Education, and Welfare on the advice of the Food and Drug Administration announced the finding of "excessive" levels of a pesticide, aminotriazole, on cranberries.

The timing of the announcement threatened to disrupt the marketing of the cranberry crop for Thanksgiving and Christmas. Presidential candidates vied with one another in defending the safety of cranberries and in announcing their intention of including them on their personal Thanksgiving menus. The public furor, and the claims and counterclaims of HEW and the Department of Agriculture, led to a request for the President's Science Advisory Committee to examine the situation.[3] One of the results was a short, publicly issued report on "Food Additives."[4] This report suggested needed areas of research and changes in administrative patterns in order to deal with chemicals and drugs as food substances. Specifically, the report called attention to the scientifically unacceptable concept of "zero tolerance" and suggested the desirability of replacing this concept with one involving finite but insignificantly small risks.[5]

In 1962, a Life Sciences Panel of the President's Science Advisory Committee began an evaluation of the use of pesticides in agriculture. The stimulus for this study came from two sources. Boisfeuillet Jones, special assistant for health and medical affairs to the Secretary of HEW, recommended through the Federal Council on Science and Technology that such a study be done. The other was the rising tide of public concern for the environment, stimulated in part by the announcement of a forthcoming book, *Silent Spring*, by Rachel Carson. The resulting report, "Use of Pesticides," was apparently instrumental in redirecting some parts of the Government's policies toward chemical pesticides.[6]

In the spring of 1964, the Office of Science and Technology and the President's Science Advisory Committee initiated, on their own, a study of environmental pollution. At roughly the same time, President Johnson was in the process of setting up a series of task forces on each of several important issues. Donald Hornig, the science adviser, persuaded a number of the White House staff that environmental pollution was an appropriate topic for inclusion among those being considered for task forces. As a result, a decision was made to adopt the PSAC Panel on Environmental Pollution as the President's Task Force. This arrangement was particularly important in brokering the information and the results of the task force's deliberations into the government agencies and into the budgetary process well before the final report was completed. As a result, many of the ideas and recommendations of this panel were translated rather readily into presidential messages to the Congress, executive orders, and budgetary submissions. Further, in contrast to some of the other task forces, a final report, "Restoring the Quality of Our Environment," was published in November 1965.[7]

One of the areas where the presidential science advisory apparatus made recommendations was the pattern and the level of research activity that it felt the government should support in behalf of the environment. In the mid-1960s, for example, the science adviser's staff persuaded the National Institutes of Health of the desirability of supporting some preliminary investigations into the potential represented by various chemicals (principally pesticides) of provoking cancer, birth defects, or genetic alteration. These experiments, eventually supported by the National Cancer Institute and known as the Bionetics experiments, were to have an importance of their own in later, governmental regulation.

The Herbicide 2, 4, 5-T

One of the first issues this writer was "handed" upon entering the Office of Science and Technology was that of the herbicide known as 2, 4, 5-T.*[8] 2, 4, 5-T, which was chemical shorthand for 2, 4, 5-trichlorophenoxyacetic acid, was developed during World War II as a result of a government fostered program designed to find suitable plant regulators for use as herbicides and defoliants. 2, 4, 5-T (along with a series of other chemical herbicides) achieved a high level of use in the United States on range-land and pasture-land, for the control of aquatic weeds and for the maintenance of rights of ways. However, the domestic use of 2, 4, 5-T was ultimately overshadowed by a heavy demand for the chemical in defoliation and crop destruction activities in the war in Southeast Asia beginning in 1962. In fact, in the face of the demand for 2, 4, 5-T in Vietnam, the domestically used quantities actually decreased by 48 percent between 1964 and 1968.

2, 4, 5-T was one of the chemical pesticides tested in the Bionetics experiments begun in 1964. Among the positive results of that screening study was the finding that 2, 4, 5-T appeared to provoke a higher than expected rate of birth defects in mice and rats when administered to those experimental animals in sufficiently high doses at appropriate periods during gestation. Although the preliminary experiments were completed in 1968, their results remained sequestered from public view for approximately 18 months. Interpretation and even the validity of these data were uncertain. The agencies responsible for regulatory action were unclear as to what they were to do in the face of these unexpected, unscheduled findings. By late 1968 and early 1969, the issue of military defoliation in Southeast Asia was beginning to arouse public controversy. Scattered, anecdotal newspaper accounts of

---

*Those interested in a more detailed account of the government's handling of the 2, 4, 5-T issue are advised to read a number of other articles and reports on this subject.

congenital abnormalities among offspring born to women in certain parts of Vietnam began to emerge. In some of these press accounts, birth defects were linked to defoliation operations.

Concurrent with the concern over military defoliation (but arousing less public notice) was a series of criticisms of herbicide use (including 2, 4, 5-T) in the Torito National Forest near Globe, Arizona. These criticisms turned around possible harm to human health and to plant and animal life.

The item which focused public attention on this issue and which forced explicit governmental action was a telephone call from Dr. Matthew Meselson, a Harvard-based scientist, to the science adviser threatening to make the results of the Bionetics study publicly available if the government did not do so itself. The government's response was swift. It included an announcement (by the science adviser, Lee DuBridge) of a series of regulatory-type, restrictive moves for various forms of the herbicide and the establishment of a panel of the President's Science Advisory Committee to review the scientific facts involved.[9] It also secured additional time for more deliberate analysis of the factual background for a more definitive set of actions. That it was the Science Adviser who made the announcement was reasonable since the issue cut across several agencies, including HEW, Agriculture, Interior, and Defense.

There were several glaring uncertainties and gaps in knowledge at the outset. The uncertainties over the Bionetics results provoked a further statistical analysis of the observed results plus some additional confirmatory experiments. The anecdotal accounts of ecological damage and congenital malformations became the subject of field studies in Southeast Asia and in Arizona. At the same time, the PSAC panel, whose chairman was Dr. Colin MacLeod, began to examine the available scientific facts. The original charter of this panel had included a review of a number of herbicides. However, the only one for which a report was published was 2, 4, 5-T.

The PSAC Panel on Herbicides studied the questions about 2, 4, 5-T in a characteristically deliberate and scientifically careful fashion. In fact, considering the pace of political events, the deliberateness seemed agonizingly slow. The DuBridge announcement in October pointed to a series of government agency restrictions on 2, 4, 5-T which would remain in effect unless evidence was obtained within two months to argue against them. The panel's study clearly would take more time. However, certain important findings did begin to fall into place by April of 1970 when a subcommittee of the Senate Commerce Committee held hearings on 2, 4, 5-T.[10] Lee DuBridge agreed to testify as director of the Office of Science and Technology. Much of his testimony reflected the findings of the PSAC panel.

The most striking finding was the great paucity of truly scientific information upon which one could assess, with confidence, the hazard 2, 4, 5-T might represent to human health. When the herbicide had been approved by the Department of Agriculture years earlier, the kinds of toxicological information demanded by the government were limited to simple studies of acute toxicity. These had indicated a material of relatively low toxicity. Over a period of twenty years, the level of understanding in science had inevitably raised the degree of sophistication of hypotheses and questions which scientists would invoke when looking into the implications of a chemical agent for human health. The Bionetics study was, in a way, a start in that direction. It was designed as a screening study, not a definitive study. From a scientist's point of view, a proper next step was to confirm and extend the Bionetics observations—most desirably through independent scientific investigations.

The biological endpoint or disease process in question in this case, teratogenesis, was a particular challenge. Many among the lay public and some scientists tended to casually group the phenomenon of congenital malformation or birth defects with the other, equally egregious phenomena, cancer and alteration in genetic material. In fact, the underlying biological mechanisms were probably entirely different. The PSAC panel discussion pointed out that teratogenesis from chemical agents was most likely an acute, toxic phenomenon with a very steep dose-response characteristic. Essentially any biologically active material, if it could cross the placental barrier separating the developing fetus from the maternal environment and if it were introduced at the right time during gestation, would be capable of disrupting the normal sequence of embryonic or fetal development. Simple tests that did not account for key variables would fail to reveal the real importance of chemicals on the human embryo. Aspirin was an exceedingly powerful teratogen in some experimental animals. Thalidomide consistently had been found to give negative results in the laboratory. Finally, the PSAC panel judged the anecdotal accounts of birth defects reported in the newspaper and elsewhere as thoroughly unreliable.

A key finding by the panel was the presence in the pesticide of an exceedingly toxic contaminant—a member of the family of dioxins. This feature became prominent in the subsequent discussions about toxicity and teratogenicity and colored the interpretation of the experimental findings.

The examination of the 2, 4, 5-T case by the Office of Science and Technology and by the PSAC panel brought forth a number of issues which were not strictly scientific but which linked scientific information to public policy. The laws governing the registration of pesticides by the Department of Agriculture were very rigid instruments. This rigidity conflicted strongly with the dynamic character of scientific discovery and understanding. As a result, there was little accommodation for a new but tentative scientific finding whose implications might be important but were not assuredly so. Armed with the results of this study, Lee DuBridge, testifying in April 1970, touched on a number of major policy and administrative questions—the cost of performing the necessary research to determine the safety of chemicals, the effect of this burden on innovation by industry toward new and improved products, the inflexibility of the law and the need for changes in the laws governing the regulation.*[11]

The report of the PSAC Panel on Herbicides was issued publicly in March 1971. Well before that date, the substantive findings of the panel and their recommendations had been shared with the agencies involved. This pattern was a common one. When the advisory process worked well, the government would already have acknowledged and put into effect the recommendations of a report before it was issued publicly. In this case, the observations made about the administratively rigid law were entered constructively into the ongoing deliberations over proposed amendments to the Federal Insecticide, Fungicide, and Rodenticide Act. The OST study did purchase some needed time for the regulatory agencies to consider the factual material and to engage some additional, needed experiments. Further, there was some coordination brought about of the review of scientific facts and the announcement of regulatory actions.

The actions by the science adviser's office on 2, 4, 5-T were without doubt useful. They were responsive to a political issue in real time. They did succeed in instilling some good scientific advice into the government's deliberations and a scientific basis for the regulatory actions. On the other hand, the growing proximity of regulatory judgment to the White House brought with it as well a degree of nervousness. Some on the White House staff were persuaded that such controversial no-win issues should be kept strictly in the agencies.

*An interesting event occurred to this author during the course of those hearings. I seated myself during one of the sessions with the group of spectators watching the hearing. In doing so, I found myself between two protagonists for opposite points of view. Independently and at separate times, the person on my right and the person on my left turned to me during the hearing to volunteer their points of view without any knowledge of my own affiliation or background. One, a pregnant mother, expressed the concern that her about-to-be delivered infant would be deformed, since she had come in contact with a weed killer containing 2, 4, 5-T. The other, a farmer, snorted that in his occupation, he had been "covered with the stuff" all his life and had suffered no ill effects. These two points of view, expressed with conviction but with essentially no scientific foundation, captured the two extremes of public thinking on this highly controversial topic.

These actions did not by any means settle the 2, 4, 5-T affair. For one thing, the various pieces of authorizing law which permitted regulatory action directed that those decisions be taken by the agencies themselves. There was a formal administrative procedure put in place by each of the regulatory agencies involved—FDA, USDA, and, later, EPA—and these had a life of their own. Nor did these decisions always square with the scientific judgments offered by the expert scientific advisers. For example, in August 1971, the administrator of EPA rejected the recommendations of his own scientific advisory committee concerned with 2, 4, 5-T and proposed a severe restriction on the use of the chemical.[12] While the restrictions were extensive, they were not absolute and a controversy over 2, 4, 5-T continues to the present day.[13]

Perhaps the most important feature of the 2, 4, 5-T story is the pattern it represented. The science adviser and his office became the recipient in the White House of a continuous series of regulatory issues where the nominal aim of the regulation in each case was protection of human health and safety. The list of regulatory issues or flaps included a series of "three letter words" that became household terms—such as DDT, PCBs, DES—as well as phosphates and enzymes in household detergents, antibiotics in animal feeds, tetraethyl lead, fluorocarbons, occupational hazards of uranium mining, and nuclear waste disposal.

These issues would reach the White House level for a number of reasons. In many cases, the issue was one that involved more than one federal agency, and a reasonably coherent government policy was desirable. The issue was often also highly visible in the public's eye and highly controversial, and there was a public demand for resolution. Often, as well, there were serious disagreements over factual material.

There were a number of common features to all of these regulatory flaps. In a very large fraction of cases, the newly raised issue represented, in fact, the reopening of an older government decision because of a new and unexpected scientific finding or a new hypothesis. 2, 4, 5-T had been registered by the Department of Agriculture in 1948 and had been considered to be a "safe" product for agricultural use. The hypothesis that 2, 4, 5-T might induce cancer or congenital anomalies or distort genetic material had simply not been considered in an earlier day, nor were there scientific insight or tools available to investigate those questions in many cases, even if they had been asked.

In one way or another, the science adviser, in each case, was asked for his judgment about the quality of the scientific information available and about the quality of the judgments offered by the advocate parties. The quality of the scientific information was almost uniformly bad. Again, one did not have to invoke a conspiratorial theory to explain the thinness of the scientific fabric for regulatory issues. Earlier government permission had been granted to companies to manufacture and market in a day when the questions about biological properties were looked upon very simply. Investigations to determine the potential to provoke cancer or birth defects were simply not considered nor demanded at the time chemical products were first passed on by the government. By the same token, except for therapeutic drugs, there was generally little or no information describing how or if an individual chemical was absorbed into the animal organism, whether it was metabolized, whether it was stored preferentially, in one or another of the body's organs, and how and at what rate it was excreted. These are elementary pieces of scientific insight that one must have in order to begin to speculate about pathological effects and hazards to health.

The scientific review in each case inevitably carried with it a series of broader questions which linked the purely scientific features to public policy questions. These eventually loomed large as the most important aspects in each case. One set concerned the matters of responsibility for gathering the scientific data on which regulatory decisions were to be based. Traditionally, for products such as pesticides and therapeutic drugs, the manufacturers undertook the investigations to supply the information to the government as a part of the general process of development of new products. With a much augmented demand for scientific insight about each product and with an increasing trend of asking for new information about older, already registered products, the cost of deriving this information appeared to be prohibitively high. Some companies began to inform the government and the science adviser of their decision to disengage from the process of innovation toward new and better products or even from the manufacture of classes of products. In a similar vein, there was heard the complaint that the U.S. regulatory obligations tended to make it more attractive for firms with multinational interests to transfer their R & D functions abroad, where the political climate was more favorable and receptive.

There were fundamental questions about just how appropriate regulation was as a means to protect human health. To what extent should decisions take account of the breadth of considerations that generally were involved by a regulatory action through what the legal system recognizes as "balancing"? Alternatively, should decisions be constrained to consider only the narrow issue of health? How could the desired process of analysis of risks and benefits be performed in the face of great uncertainty (about both risks and benefits)? Again, how much scientific information was enough? For pharmaceutical products, for example, how much laboratory investigation should be completed before beginning testing in humans? When should marketing begin and what obligations should there be for postmarketing surveillance?

Chemicals and Health

These broad public policy questions, partly scientific, partly legal, partly administrative, and partly economic in character, began to emerge more and more sharply from the series of specific regulatory issues. As a result, it was the judgment of the Office of Science and Technology that the time was particularly ripe to engage a broad and intensive review of important aspects of the regulatory activities of the government aimed at the protection of human health and safety. In a purely political sense, this was a risky venture. The political tide of environmentalists' concerns was still rising sharply and the administration was only too eager to embrace it. Several new agencies or rearrangements of the government designed to foster regulation were born out of this tide of political enthusiasm. The Council on Environmental Quality was brought into being in January 1970. In the same year, new occupational safety and health legislation was passed establishing a new infrastructure for industrial health concerns and the Environmental Protection Agency was established. The Consumer Product Safety Commission was created in 1972, almost enveloping the FDA in the process.

Yet, from a scientific and a science-for-policy point of view, it appeared clear in 1970 that serious distortions would occur in how science was to be used for important and far-reaching government decisions if special attention were not given to this difficult field or regulation. Accordingly, there was mounted in the Office of Science and Technology a complementary series of exercises and studies between 1970 and 1973, all directed at this general field of interest:

1. In 1971, the Office of Science and Technology undertook with the cooperation and collaboration of certain of the agencies, an analysis of the combined regulatory impact and the benefits of various automobile emission control strategies and various mandated automotive safety features.[14]

2. In 1971 and 1972, the Office of Science and Technology in collaboration with the Council on Environmental Quality undertook a thorough review of all of the federal programs of research into the effects of environmental materials on human health.[15]

3. Beginning in 1972, OST engaged a group of outside experts as a "Panel on Hazardous Trace Substances" to advise on the research needs of the government to assure an adequate understanding of substances which existed in man's environment in trace quantities. This panel, which worked for over a year, undertook three case studies as a vehicle for studying the problem. In the case of one of these, polychlorinated biphenyls, the panel's findings eventually became the principal substantive material on which the government based its regulatory decisions.[16]

4. In early 1970, a panel of the President's Science Advisory Committee was established to examine in depth the many issues raised in the government's concerns for the effect of chemical substances on human health. The chairman of the Panel on Chemicals and Health was John Tukey who, five years before, had served as the chairman of the PSAC Panel on Environmental Pollution. The terms of reference for this panel made no mention of government regulation. However, since regulation was effectively the sole vehicle used by the government to control environmental chemicals, that clearly was a major focus of the study.

The PSAC Panel on Chemicals and Health had a carefully chosen membership designed to reflect the breadth of the policy issues to be discussed. Included were two economists, two lawyers, two chemists, a pharmacologist, a statistician, and two representatives of industry, as well as two experts in environmental health. The chairman also took pains to engage as advisers to the panel, senior spokesmen from each of the principal federal agencies involved and the president of the National Academy of Sciences. This was aimed at facilitating the brokering of the ideas developed by the panel into the thinking and planning in the government departments.

The Panel on Chemicals and Health received an enormous amount of testimony from a great variety of spokesmen on all sides of health and regulatory issues—industry executives, biological scientists, consumerists and other public interest groups, lawyers, and economists. Delegations were dispatched abroad to study regulatory patterns in several parts of Western Europe and the United Kingdom.

Notably, certain major public policy questions were addressed. One, for example, was the amount of safety or freedom from risk the nation desired and secured through regulation. The contribution to morbidity and mortality occasioned by exposure to various chemical substances was compared to risks assumed by people in other settings. The panel, in this way, observed that absolute freedom from risk was not a realistic possibility.

The panel (as might be expected) strongly urged that the government rest its regulatory decisions on a firmer scientific base. There were both private and public responsibilities, it was felt, for substantially strengthening that base. Public accountability for government decisions was important and government had a responsibility to make explicit and detailed explanations for the reasons behind the decisions.

The work was a massive one. The panel concluded with ten Principles, twenty-three General Recommendations, and fifty-three Specific Recommendations (divided into various categories).[17] Its scope was enormous. There were detailed recommendations about how much and what kinds of scientific research the government should support. The Delaney Amendment to the Food, Drug, and Cosmetic Act was addressed ("A 'no-detectable amount' clause is a refuge in the face of ignorance.").[18] There were responsibilities described for scientists, government, and the press to assist in public education about health and regulatory matters.

There were admonitions to the Congress ("National policy needs to give the most attention to the largest threats to health, even if these threats have been frequently recognized.")[19] The "largest" threats to health were clearly cigarettes and alcohol. Balancing in the decision making was said to be clearly in the national interest, as was diversity in the products and material available for public consumption.[20]

Here was clearly a document that was public policy oriented and far from the mold of traditional science advisory products. The panel's deliberations and analyses became highly influential in steering the course of certain of the Government's activities.* Research budgets for environmental health, which had overwhelmingly favored radiation biology, were augmented in order to provide for the study of chemical agents. A number of legislative initiatives—amendments to the Food, Drug and Cosmetic Act and the federal pesticide law, for example—were shaped in part because of this study. The government's concerns for the economic impact of regulation were heightened and eventually treated more systematically. The report remains an authority and continues to be prominently cited in current discussions of health-related regulatory issues.[21]

On the other hand, this exercise was not embraced immediately with overwhelming enthusiasm by others on the White House staff. Once again, it had no patron. The task was undertaken at the initiative of OST and with the knowledge (but not at the invitation) of the President. It dealt with a subject which was, by its nature, controversial. As the Watergate revelations emerged, the President's own staff was more and more inclined to embrace "safe" areas.

---

*The panel and staff produced a large series of background documents and analyses during the course of this study.

Perhaps as important as anything else, the general subject of the panel's work was ahead of its time. Regulatory reform was not to become a legitimate subject for government interest for another two years. Finally, under the circumstances of the time, the panel was perhaps more dilatory in completing its study than it should have been. By the time the report was released publicly and the panel had presented its findings in a public press conference (a usual event for the President's Science Advisory Committee), the President had translated the science adviser's post to the director of the National Science Foundation and had disenfranchised the President's Science Advisory Committee.

Legislation and Government Reorganization

The Office of Science and Technology registered its point of view on legislative proposals principally via the legislative clearance function of the Office of Management and Budget. This was a forum designed to collect systematically the points of view of all of the agencies of the executive branch on legislative initiatives, both those that had originated in the Congress and those that began in the executive branch. In addition, certain legislative proposals, such as the Toxic Substances Control Act, actually had their origin in the science adviser's office.

The early 1970s were marked by extensive legislative activity and administrative reorganization designed to reshape the governmental fabric in behalf of environmental and consumer betterment. In great part, this was a response to a popular sentiment to utilize the leverage of government where private market activity was deficient. In part, too, it was symptomatic of an ever-present competition between the executive and the legislative branches over which would gain the most public credit for having moved the government structure the greatest distance in behalf of the environment.

One of the most important and far-reaching of the legislative initiatives of the era was the series of 1970 amendments to the Clean Air Act.[22] The first federal legislation aimed at air pollution had been passed in 1955.[23] The initial role for the federal government had been an exceedingly modest one—a *temporary* program of research, training, and demonstration. Passage of this law had been aided politically by an air pollution episode in Donora, Pennsylvania. Another severe air pollution episode in 1962, in London, England, gave Congress additional impetus to pass the Clean Air Act a year later. Within two more years, a series of amendments to the Clean Air Act were passed that, for the first time, recognized the sizable contribution of automotive exhaust to urban air pollution.[24] The committee report that accompanied the bill on its way to the Senate floor pointed out that "the Committee believes that exact standards need not be written legislatively but that the Secretary (of HEW) should adjust to changing technology."[25] Further, in setting emission standards, the secretary was directed to give "an appropriate consideration to technological feasibility and economic costs."[26]

This philosophy was interesting, as it would be substantially reversed within less than five years. The Senate Public Works Committee and its chairman, Senator Muskie, provoked a major change in thinking about the government's role in air pollution by introducing a series of amendments to the Clean Air Act in 1969. In part, these were a product of some impatience with the pace of national progress toward solving air pollution. In part, they took advantage in timing of the public's favorable attitude toward environmental problems generally. The change in philosophy represented by these legislative proposals was enormous. The government—in fact, the Congress—was to establish the standards for automotive emissions leaving no place for administrative flexibility or discretion. Primary ambient air quality standards were to be established *exclusively* on the basis of protection of human health. There would be no room for consideration of economic costs or technical feasibility. In the face of considerable ignorance, the relationship between emissions and ambient air levels of contaminants was assumed to be a proportional one—an assumption that had very little scientific support. Further, the assumed linkages between exposure to air pollutants and human disease had very limited support in valid scientific evidence.

Very little active opposition arose to this legislation. The automotive industry argued (although not convincingly) that the proposed legislation could not be met in technical terms. The Office of Science and Technology considered the concept of mandatory standards as bad public policy and the particular values chosen for adoption as emission standards were thought to be scientifically indefensible. Furthermore, OST argued that the proposed accelerated schedule for implementing the emission standards would be exceedingly expensive to accommodate and would not bring about a commensurate reduction in ambient air pollution, because of the interacting variables of new cars introduced into use, old cars still in use, other sources of air pollutants, problems of maintenance of emission control devices, and uncertainty over the relationships between emissions and ambient air quality.[27]

In spite of this advice, there was little receptivity to contrary arguments to this legislation. The political momentum was too strong and the political desire for identification and alignment with environmental issues was too prominent to accommodate scientific factual information of a contrary sort.

Another year would pass before the White House would begin to question the wisdom of uncritical adoption of the Clean Air Act amendments of 1970, and then the key issue would be the economic consequences of their implementation.

The Toxic Substances Control Act, passed by Congress in 1976,[28] was in great part the product of a concept born in the staff of the science adviser. Regulation of pesticides was in the hands of the Department of Agriculture with specific assistance from the Food and Drug Administration. The law which authorized that regulatory activity was to receive some useful amendments, as a result, in part, of the experience with 2, 4, 5-T. The Food and Drug Administration, as well as exercising responsibilities for pharmaceutical products and food substances, also possessed mild authority over a less clearly defined class of substances known as "hazardous materials." This authority, known as the Hazardous Substances Act,[29] directed the government to proceed against chemical materials whose labeling did not adequately reflect the degree of hazard which the substance represented.*

Following a trip to Sweden in 1970, where he had participated in a meeting on chemicals in the environment, one of the members of the staff of the Office of Science and Technology observed in a memorandum that the government suffered a gap in its coverage of chemical substances which could become environmental contaminants.[30] Essentially, this gap was the large class of industrial chemical substances that were used as chemical intermediates and served as the basic materials for the manufacture of thousands of chemical substances and products sold in the retail market place. The real challenge and the government's most pronounced need, it was felt, was for a way to inform itself about what specific chemical substances within this class were manufactured in what quantities and where they flowed in the complex labyrinth of commerce. The air and water pollution laws permitted the government to gather some information about chemicals as they appeared as effluents and emissions. Certain key chemical product classes (such as pesticides and drugs) were regulated. When substantial accidents occurred in the bulk handling of chemicals, there was in place at least a loose reporting system. However, there was no avenue available to the federal government to advise itself routinely and systematically about the basic details of this large category of industrial level chemicals which clearly represented the bulk of the U.S. chemical production.

From this early idea came an agreement in principle with the newly formed Council on Environmental Quality to develop a legislative instrument

---

*In fact, this law had formerly been known as the Hazardous Substances Labelling Act.

to accommodate this need. An early proposal was to utilize the existing authority of the Hazardous Substances Act. However, that law was thought of as too limited in its scope. Further, the responsibility for administering that law lay with the Food and Drug Administration and the set of questions for toxic substances seemed to require an agency with a broader view. The first draft of the Toxic Substances Control Act was notable for the fact that its major purpose was to inform the government, although it contained mild and simple regulatory powers.[31] Interestingly, the Office of Science and Technology together with the Council on Environmental Quality was able to derive presidential support for this legislation in numerous public statements, presidential messages to Congress,[32] and reports to the Congress.[33] The Toxic Substances Control Act was finally enacted into law in 1976.[34] The final version was a substantially different bill than the original. It was much more complex, much more difficult to administer, and clearly more of a regulatory instrument than an informational tool.

The major administrative changes in behalf of environmental quality were the establishment of the staff-level Council on Environmental Quality and the amalgamation of regulatory activities in a new Environmental Protection Agency. EPA was in part the product of a study of executive branch organization by the Ash Council.* The new conglomerate that became EPA was an attempt to place under one administrative roof all of the major regulatory and standard-setting activities for the environment. These activities were formerly scattered among other agencies—Interior, HEW, Agriculture, the AEC. This move was also responsive to a general public mood in favor of separating regulatory and protection-related functions from those responsible for promotion and development.[35] OST was a member of the Ash Council and, hence, contributed to this process.

The evolution of the Council on Environmental Quality had a different sort of history. In May 1969, President Nixon established by Executive Order an Environmental Quality Council and a Citizens' Advisory Committee on Environmental Quality.[36] The spirit behind this move was to give attention to environmental matters at the White House Level and to signal that concern publicly. This organization was to be parallel to an Urban Affairs Council and the National Security Council. The members of the council were cabinet secretaries and the vice president. The science adviser was designated as the

*President's Advisory Council on Executive Organization: Mr. Roy Ash, who had been the president of Litton Industries, was later to become the director of the Office of Management and Budget. The Ash Council was an ad hoc group directed to examine certain organizational aspects of the executive branch.

executive secretary and the Office of Science and Technology was to act as the staff for its functions. The Council was to meet monthly and a series of task forces on specific issues—transportation and handling of hazardous substances, handling of waste materials, automotive pollution, noise—was set up using members of various government agencies.

The Congress, however, not willing to be outdone, proceeded on its own toward legislation to establish in the Executive Office of the President a Council on Environmental Quality. It was the White House's hope that the existing Environmental Quality Council would satisfy the congressional mood and serve their desire for an environmental focus in the White House. However, these arguments were not specifically convincing and on January 1, 1970, the National Environmental Policy Act was passed giving a statutory basis to the Council on Environmental Quality and establishing a complex and far-reaching reporting procedure on environmental issues.*[37]

When the Congress legislated the institutional focus for the environment in the President's office, his own, cabinet-level organization ceased to function. Nominally, the work of the task forces of the Environmental Quality Council was to be directed in behalf of the new CEQ.[38] However, as an entity, the Environmental Quality Council ceased to have an identity of its own. This pattern of "spinning off" functions from the science adviser's office to discrete and dedicated institutions within the Executive Office was not unknown. Two earlier examples of note were the National Space Council and the National Council on Marine Resources and Engineering Development. With time, the functions served by these new organizations ceased to warrant separate offices and their responsibilities were returned to the Office of Science and Technology. A later development of the same sort, a Federal Energy Office, would ultimately be replaced by an entirely new, cabinet-level agency, a Department of Energy.

The statutory basis for the Council on Environmental Quality did not by any means guarantee the persuasion of the incumbent President on specific environmental issues and, at times, the council's advice was actively ignored. However, the CEQ, particularly because of the unusual reporting obligations of the National Environmental Policy Act, has served as a visible focus for environmental interests. The continuing function of the science adviser's office has been a complementary one directed principally at the scientific and technical issues involved in environmental problems and projects.

---

*In fact, two laws were passed simultaneously—one establishing the Council on Environmental Quality and the other providing for the staff of the CEQ.

Quality of Life Review Process

One of the most striking and most direct forms of involvement of the science advisory apparatus in the public policy machinery was the establishment of the "Quality of Life Review Process." In 1969 and 1970, the series of new legislative proposals for augmented environmental and health regulation were generally warmly accepted by the White House. Although a few voices of concern were raised about elements of the Clean Air Act amendments in 1969, no substantial objections or reservations were sustained.

However, early in 1971, concern began to mount in various industrial sectors and within the Commerce Department over the costs to industry of implementing the new laws. In addition, it became evident to some (who should have realized the fact before) that explicit balancing among the various costs and benefits and the effects on other governmental and national programs and policies when reaching certain important regulatory and standard-setting decisions was not possible and, in fact, clearly enjoined by the Clean Air Act. These factors of high apparent costs to industry and to the public resulting from the law plus an inability to explore systematically the broad implications of a regulation created a serious degree of frustration within the executive branch. The lack of a systematic examination of costs and benefits in each case particularly concerned economists and persons responsible for budget decisions.

The Commerce Department, led by its secretary, Maurice Stans, championed a position that generally found regulations offensive and costly. Stans established within the Commerce Department the National Industrial Pollution Control Council—a vehicle to invite industrial points of view on regulatory matters.

Partly as a result of their frustration with the severe limitations set by regulatory laws, and partly due to large budgetary requests made to OMB by EPA, George Schultz, then director of the Office of Management and Budget, directed a memorandum to the administrator of EPA in which he expressed concern for the incomplete understanding about both costs and benefits of proposed environmental regulation.[39] Notably, the memorandum expressed the intent of OMB to review and clear regulatory proposals in much the same way that it did for legislative and budgetary proposals.

Within less than a month, symptomatic of the degree of frustration being felt within the White House, the President directed members of his Domestic Council (essentially the members of his cabinet) to consider pointedly whether or not an institutionalized method of regular review of proposed regulatory decisions should not be instituted. The memorandum that introduced this subject began by noting that:

On a daily basis in your capacity as a Department or Agency head each of you must make decisions that affect the balance of many Quality of Life variables—particularly consumer and environmental interests, industrial requirements, and safety aspects—some decisions working to the disadvantage of others. The President has directed that a study be undertaken of this balance to determine . . . whether a government vehicle (for example, a small permanent group) should be established to review decisions affecting this balance.[40]

Among the addressees, in addition to the cabinet secretaries, were Mrs. Virginia Knauer, special assistant to the President for consumer affairs; Peter Peterson, presidential assistant for international economic affairs; William Ruckelshaus, administrator of EPA; and Russell Train, chairman of the CEQ. Edward David, the President's science adviser, was named as chairman of a committee to consider the general challenge of this memorandum and was given roughly three weeks to deliver a reply.

The issues behind this memorandum had developed to a high point in only a short period of time. In July 1971, Secretary of Commerce Stans delivered his famous "Wait a Minute" speech in which he admonished the country to exercise caution before dedicating itself overwhelmingly to environmental concerns.[41] This speech corresponded roughly in time with a "battle of briefs"—a virtual cross fire of memoranda and position papers from various agency heads to the President, each representing an authoritative point of view on the economic consequences of the Clean Air Act standards and regulations.[42] These memoranda from Stans; Russell Train, chairman of the Council on Environmental Quality; and Paul McCracken, chairman of the Council of Economic Advisers, inevitably disagreed sharply with each other. The tone of the President's reaction to his chairman of the Council on Environmental Quality can be sensed from his instruction transmitted by his staff secretary, Jon Huntsman:

While the President read with interest Mr. Whitaker's memorandum of July 1, 1971, containing Russell Train's memorandum of June 30, 1971, it was noted that he did not believe Mr. Train's analysis. It was requested that you obtain for the President's review an *honest* and unbiased report by someone other than an environmentalist.[43]

The agency spokesmen called to consider this presidential proposal for a "small permanent group to review decisions" were generally sympathetic to the need to address the balancing question. They generally agreed that it was in the national interest to broaden the agenda of review for regulatory decisions. However, there was serious anxiety over the appropriateness of lifting regulatory matters out of the agencies assigned that responsibility by Congress. Further, there was concern over the legality of interjecting analysis and comments *in camera* outside the statutorily provided avenues for public information and public comment. There was fear, too, that the volume of regulatory proposals that might come to a centrally located review group would overwhelm that office and, therefore, a centrally located analytic resource might fare no better than the agencies' own resources.

The science adviser himself sensed the serious political hazards of the basic proposal. Although he was not able to escape the task of exploring the issue as he had been directed, he indicated little enthusiasm for running the review process from his office. His staff did undertake the majority of the planning and, in collaboration with others on the White House staff, designed a relatively simple mechanism for systematic agency review of regulatory issues before they were formally proposed in the Federal Register.[44] The mechanism had two parts: agencies were to send to the Office of Management and Budget (the "manager" of the Quality of Life Review Process) a schedule a year in advance of important regulatory decisions and, for each of them, an analysis which included specific features in each case. The OMB, as the recipient of these analyses, would act as the convener of meetings to bring the interested agencies together to express their comments and recommendations for each regulatory proposal.

The Quality of Life Review Process was interesting in several respects. It was nominally applied to all agencies which had regulatory and standards-setting responsibilities within the executive branch. (OST had developed a detailed analysis of its own of all of the health- and safety-related laws, the degrees of discretion and timetables dictated by Congress and the agencies responsible for carrying out the mandates.) In practice, however, with one exception, the Quality of Life Review Process was applied exclusively to the EPA.

William Ruckelshaus, administrator of EPA, saw positive benefit to his agency in receiving comments from other parts of the federal government on EPA's proposed actions. However, he was offended by the process, which was to be managed by the Office of Management and Budget. He succeeded in avoiding any formal "clearance" process and, by 1977, the agency unilaterally terminated its participation in the Quality of Life Review Process.

As a footnote, it is interesting to note that, for essentially the same reasons—a desire to broaden the basis of regulatory decisions and frustration over the agencies' inability or unwillingness to do this themselves—a "central" review process has continued. Currently, a Regulatory Analysis Group, directed by the Council of Economic Advisers, established by an Executive Order,[45] receives a schedule of proposed, important regulatory and standard-setting actions (Regulatory Calendar) and reviews the analyses submitted by the agencies in each case. The essential distinction between this arrangement and the Quality of Life Review Process is the point in the administrative process where the centrally directed review is inserted. Where the Quality of Life Review Process exercised its review before the period of public comment on a regulatory proposal, the Regulatory Analysis Group inserts its results *following* the period of public comment in each case. A fundamental question of jurisdiction of the President and his office to comment on and interact with the business of regulatory agencies remains and is the subject of current discussion[46] and challenges[47] from outside the government.

Swords to Plowshares

In November 1969, President Nixon renounced the use, development, procurement, and stockpiling of weapons of biological warfare. Remaining research would be directed toward defensive measures such as immunization. The administration desired to demonstrate its strong support for the Geneva Protocol early in its term, and public support was needed for prompt Senate ratification.

As a result of this decision, the government's research and development program and its tools of production of biological warfare agents were to be rapidly phased down. There suddenly became available three substantial facilities, Hunter's Point, California; Pine Bluff, Arkansas; and Fort Dietrich, Maryland. These extensive facilities were rendered surplus overnight. In February 1970, the President asked Lee DuBridge, the science adviser, to advise him if there were any suitable scientific uses to which any of these facilities could be put.[48]

There were, not unexpectedly, factors that needed to be considered and several interests which had to be satisfied. One was the necessity of identifying tasks of true scientific merit for which these facilities were particularly suited. It was felt important that any new scientific program for these facilities be clearly understood as unrelated to any military purpose and that it be openly available to cooperating scientists throughout the world. At the same time, one of the panels of the President's Science Advisory Committee urged that specific aspects of the former biological warfare research program concerned with *defense* and *protection* against microbiological agents be continued. This would mean setting aside a portion of the physical facilities at Fort Dietrich to remain in the jurisdiction of the Army. There was an additional challenge concerning the continued employment of the existing staffs. The Army employed at both Pine Bluff and at Fort Dietrich very large numbers of civilians. The congressional delegations from both Maryland and Arkansas became mobilized soon after the original announcement to persuade the federal government not only to find alternative uses for the physical plants but to retrain and continue the employment of the existing professional and supporting staffs.[49] Finally, the budget support for any new program would necessarily have to come from the adopting agency which assumed the facilities. This quickly became a particular problem since, at the same time, the ground rules for the President's budget threatened to restrict expenditures. Budgetary support would have to be taken away from other, already existing programs.

None of the facilities was immediately translatable into new lines of biomedical research. The Fort Dietrich laboratories had been used in great part for applied studies related to the development of biological warfare agents. The facilities at Pine Bluff contained very large-scale apparatus used in the actual production of microbiological agents. All of the facilities were relatively isolated physically from established academic and medical research centers.

The OST staff began immediately to explore with various agencies—especially HEW and USDA—the possibilities for new scientific uses. An early, formal response from Robert Finch, secretary of HEW, to Lee DuBridge expressed confidence that HEW could find suitable uses for one or other of the facilities if adequate funding could be found. Finch's proposal was that the Army underwrite the support of some of the employees in the new program[50]—a proposal that was less than totally acceptable to the Army.

The staff of OST took note of a recommendation made by a group of outside advisers to the FDA for a government-sponsored research project designed to explore the effects of very low doses of chemical substances. The proposal called for chronic exposure of very large numbers of animals under rigorously controlled conditions from which it was hoped important general principles of dose-response relationships could be derived.[51] The science adviser's office requested that the group of advisers who had recommended this specific project visit the facilities to ascertain if any of them were suitable for the "megamouse" experiments. The judgment of this "visitation team" was that the Pine Bluff facilities were particularly suited for this project, although new construction and a new professional staff would be required.[52]

Robert Finch wrote to Lee DuBridge on June 5, 1970, that his agency had an "urgent need" for the Pine Bluff facility for a project to evaluate the health hazards of toxic chemicals and wished to have $7 million transferred from the Defense Department to support the program.[53] In spite of this seeming agreement, there followed a period of four months of bureaucratic wrangling during which no firm decision could be reached. At one point, it appeared that no new program could be brought about. A part of the disagreement surrounded the question of sources of funds. Another was a jurisdictional question. By this time, the new Environmental Protection Agency was established and that agency began to evince interest in running the Pine Bluff facilities (thereby giving HEW an added incentive to reconsider the project). It was OST's judgment that the project would fare best and would attract the best scientific minds if it were operated by HEW—particularly by the National Institutes of Health.[54] In this, the science adviser was able to persuade the Office of Management and Budget.[55]

Because of the inability to gain a consensus from HEW on their use of Pine Bluff, OST asked to meet in October 1970 with all of the interested agencies within that department. The meeting, held in the Office of the Assistant Secretary for Health, rapidly brought forth some important agreements. HEW concurred in the importance of the research project for large-scale testing of environmental chemicals and expressed an institutional desire to be responsible for the program. At the same time, the institute directors from NIH, to a man, declined to involve the NIH, while Charles Edwards, commissioner of the FDA, agreed to support the program. In the end, a cooperative agreement was worked out between FDA and EPA to share in the cost of the facility and its research program.

With concurrence of the agencies and OMB in place at last, a final task was to announce the transfer of Pine Bluff publicly. For this, OST wrote a public statement and draft press release for the White House. The effect of this was to name the new institution the National Center for Toxicological Research and to provide a statement from the presidential level as to its charter. An anecdote accompanying this modest task is illustrative of the relations between an advisory office and the public policy machinery. The draft press release began, "Dr. Edward E. David, Jr., Director of the Office of Science and Technology, announced today that a new, major project aimed at investigating the health effects of a variety of chemicals will be established in the surplus biological facilities of the Pine Bluff Arsenal, Pine Bluff, Arkansas." In less than an hour, the press release was returned from the President's office, approved and unchanged except that a new beginning, reading "The President . . . ," was substituted for the reference to the science adviser. Edward David was furious over the change. More seasoned hands understood that he had gained full "inside" credit for having developed an initiative thought important enough for the President to take credit.

The saga of Fort Dietrich was a much more prolonged one. In spite of the hot breath of political pressures to "re-program" the facility, in spite of the symbolic advantages to the administration in its international relations, the principal agency interested in the facility, HEW, could not easily accommodate the project. Again, the obvious department to use the facility, NIH, was wary or even reluctant to associate its traditional research with a formerly war-related scientific establishment. The National Institutes of Health stood firm in their stand against borrowing from any of the existing budgets. As a result, a bluffing game developed between the DOD and HEW. The Defense Department threatened to close the facility, and set dates for closing. HEW agreed to assume it on the condition that DOD funds could be used to support it. This latter idea even became the subject of a legislative proposal introduced by Senator Joseph Tydings.[56]

The augmented National Cancer Program finally provided the text for HEW's (and NIH's) decision to use the Fort Dietrich facilities. There was suddenly a great deal of new money. Some of the tasks (such as the cancer bioassay program) were clearly applied in character and required extensive physical facilities. Further, by delaying the decision effectively an entire fiscal year, the limiting budgetary restraints were no longer quite so severe. In June 1971, Elliot Richardson, secretary of HEW, wrote to John Ehrlichman to make known his agency's "new" position on accepting the Fort Dietrich facility.[57] It still required another five months to place the understanding on a sufficiently firm footing to permit a public announcement. In this case, the President made a personal visit by helicopter to Fort Dietrich to make the announcement.

6. POPULATION AND FAMILY PLANNING

Background

I t had been traditional in political circles to consider the related issues of population growth and family planning as untouchables. On the one hand, these were personal and family matters, not proper items for the state to consider. They would inevitably arouse strong emotions with strong religious and social overtones. From a politician's viewpoint, they were among those "no-win" issues where public identification with a point of view could be tantamount to political suicide.

The federal government, indeed, already had a modest investment in population matters. There existed a relatively small research effort within the National Institutes of Health. For population matters and assistance in family planning abroad (by far the "safer" area politically) AID had an ongoing program to promote and to educate in behalf of contraception and family planning.

The pre-inaugural task force reports on health and on science had touched on population and family planning. However, the discussions were not prominent in either case. In the report of the pre-inaugural task force on health, family planning was afforded a brief paragraph as a "longer-range special problem."[1] The corresponding discussion in the science and technology task force report was carefully academic, referred exclusively to the "world" population problem and spoke to the particular contribution that one could expect from research and from universities.[2]

Early in 1969, one of the members of the science adviser's staff addressed a memorandum to the Science Adviser suggesting that the population issue was worthy of presidential attention, that the political timing was particularly ripe for presidential attention, and that the Office of Science and Technology could make a useful contribution in formulating a governmental role. Lee DuBridge, then the science adviser, raised this idea informally with Pat Moynihan, then a counsellor to the President with special interests in social and welfare areas. Independently, Arthur Burns, also at that time a counsellor to the President, urged presidential attention to population and family planning issues. The idea that the political timing was particularly ripe, that population was no longer a politically suicidal issue, was immediately appealing to Moynihan. He persuaded the President of this point of view and successfully argued for a sequence of political events which were designed to give national prominence to the issue and to indicate the President's personal concern and attention.

The immediate vehicle was a presidential message on population to the Congress.[3] Having put the wheels in motion in behalf of that initiative, OST's further contributions to the presidential message were made in league with several other parties who were gathered together specifically in behalf of that exercise. As so often happens in instances of this sort, a small working group of about fifteen persons was assembled to gather ideas and to draft portions of a text that would eventually become a presidential pronouncement. The organizer of this task force was Patrick Moynihan, with the assistance of Philander Claxton, borrowed from the State Department to take charge of this initiative.

The message was remarkably bold and explicit for documents of this sort. It spoke to questions of both worldwide population growth and population growth in the United States. It stopped short (as it was designed to do) of articulating specific limits to population numbers or rate of growth but it clearly leaned in the direction of limiting growth. From a policy point of view, it leaned heavily on the concept of making available, through education and the techniques of contraception, the opportunity of limiting family size to all of those who desired it.

The message announced a limited number of very specific government initiatives. It called for an increase in research in behalf of improved methods of contraception. It announced a directed plan of family planning services to accommodate a target population of five million low-income women of childbearing age. It called for additional effort to train personnel to work in population and family planning areas—domestically and abroad. In addition to these specific initiatives, the message cleverly sought to share the political heat that would come from wading into the morass of population and family planning. The President called upon the *Congress* to create, by statute, a study commission to inquire into the series of important issues that are fundamental to any serious attempt to deal with a population policy.

Administratively, the federal establishment had, by virtue of previous modest steps, already moved in the direction of meeting the challenge of population and family planning. A Center for Population Research had been established in one of the institutes of NIH—the National Institute for Child Health and Human Development. (This institute was eventually to embrace a combined set of research responsibilities including aging, child health, and contraceptive research—a feature which bothered each of the related constituencies considerably.) The goal of increased family planning research was to build on the strengths already in existence in the NIH. The targeted services for low-income families were to be provided from elsewhere in HEW. For this, a new, dedicated organization, a National Center for Family Planning Services, was established in October 1969.

The Congress obliged the President with not one but two pieces of legislation. The Family Planning Services and Population Research Act of 1970 gave the President all he requested in the way of financial authorization for population services and research.[4] It put into statutory form the administrative alterations which both the incumbent and the previous Presidents had brought about. It also established, via statute, a position of deputy assistant secretary for population affairs whose task it was to provide some coordination of the population services and research activities of the federal agencies—principally AID and HEW. This last provision was to prove to be an important item. With the passage of years, the public and congressional fervor for population matters would wane. Because of the unique statutory basis for this position, there were no successful attempts to reduce its authority or to remove the incumbent from office.

The second piece of legislation established the Commission on Population Growth and the American Future.[5] This Commission was to report both to the Congress and to the President—once midway through its deliberations and again at the end of its two-year life. The chairman was to be John D. Rockefeller III, and the membership was to include two members from each of the lower and upper houses of Congress. The staff, which would eventually number forty-eight, was directed by Charles Westhoff of Princeton, and would ultimately produce a highly creditable report.[6] The commission's work was backed up and informed by a series of ninety-seven scholarly background papers ranging from energy needs and population growth to abortion.

The Science Adviser's Role during the Time of the
Population Commission

In the major policy areas concerned with population and family planning, the principal focus remained with the commission during 1971 and early 1972. During this period, OST assumed its very traditional role of concern for research and for federal funds to support it. The research program of NIH and of AID came under review by the science adviser's office with each budget season and at several intervals in between. The aims of these reviews were to consider the scientific quality of these programs, to determine if they had sound scientific merit and to consider whether their level of support corresponded to the strength of the commitment raised by the presidential announcement. Consistently through this period, the NIH program, which was of substantially better scientific quality, enjoyed relatively less support in Congress than the more flamboyant yet less scientifically worthy research effort of AID. Population matters abroad were always "safer" areas politically than were population concerns at home. Hence, there was always a warm place in congressional hearts for the AID program.

One particular aspect of the NIH research program was unusual in its departure from a traditional research role for that institution (and for the civilian side of the government). One of the philosophic aims of the contraceptive research programs of NIH was to foster the evolution of improved and safer contraceptive methods. It appeared to NIH that there existed some scientific avenues and ideas which were promising and ripe for further exploration—sometimes at a pace even faster than the private pharmaceutical industry was proceeding. Accordingly, it was decided early in the program that the National Institute of Child Health and Human Development would support a series of investigations as being appropriate and dictated by the state of scientific understanding in each case, namely, basic research, applied research, and *frank development* of contraceptive methods. This pattern had been common for years in the defense and aerospace sectors but it was all but unknown in the purely domestic arena. This latter tactic was strongly opposed by members of the pharmaceutical industry who feared their loss of patent and market positions. However, the fact remained that this government program promised to move the course of contraceptive development faster than if left entirely in the hands of the private sector. During these years, in the course of periodic budget reviews, OST successfully defended this program against critics and snipers who threatened to compromise its support.

However, it was in the follow-up to the commission's work that the science adviser's contribution to government thinking on population and family planning was again prominent. The commission had left behind nearly seventy recommendations covering a very wide swath of activities and interests. They were aimed at different levels of national action—federal, state, and local governments and segments of the private sector. Within two days of the presentation of the commission's final report, Russell Train, chairman of the Council on Environmental Quality, recommended to the President's staff that his organization be responsible for reviewing the commission's recommendations.[7] His offer was to lead and coordinate an interagency review of the commission's recommendations that affected the federal government.

The CEQ's credibility was not high within the White House structure. It represented a sizable amorphous and vocal constituency but one that was increasingly hostile to the ideas and ways of the administration. Further, the work of CEQ came to be less and less trusted by the White House, which was fearful of its intrinsic biases. Russell Train's offer was not accepted. In its place, the President asked his science adviser to review the commission's recommendations and to prepare positions for the White House. The memorandum soliciting this assistance did request that Edward David, the science adviser, "discuss the scope of work and agency participation with Chairman Train whose staff has already done some preliminary work."[8]

This, then, became the basis for yet another review of the major population issues. It was to last approximately six months. It was systematic and thorough. A number of participants were involved. Its net effect, however, was effectively to bury the issues raised by the commission from further political visibility.

The members of the "Executive Office Task Force" to consider the Population Commission's report included Ray Waldmann, a spokesman from the White House Domestic Council staff who had been working with the National Goals staff; Jack W. Carlson, of the Office of Management and Budget; June A. O'Neill, from the Council of Economic Advisers; and J. Clarence Davies III, of the Council on Environmental Quality. The ground rules were to consider what the President should do and say about the commission recommendations which related to the federal government. The Congress had clearly given the commission a broader charter of investigation than had the President in his Population Message. However, even without that, it was likely that any reasonable commission would have drawn broad rather than narrow boundaries around its tasks.

The most difficult of the recommendations with which to deal (because it was the most fundamental) was that which urged the nation to "welcome and plan for a stabilized population."[9] This raised the question of whether a proper response would be one that focused primarily on the *implications* of anticipated population growth or on measures designed primarily to *reduce* growth. It was to the former idea that the President's population message had been directed. The commission, however, stepped much further out in front by advocating ("welcoming") a pattern of reduced growth.

The other issues raised by the commission which were of particular difficulty were those about which the President had already established a public position. Notable among these were the public financing and encouragement of abortion and the availability of contraceptive information and services to minors. There had been several minority views expressed by commissioners on both of these topics. Nevertheless, the majority favored these recommendations and they stood in bold relief—clashing with presidential pronouncements a relatively short time before. In addition to these, presidential positions had already been taken prior to the release of the commission's report on certain other issues, and these would inevitably color the final White House reflection of the recommendations. Among these were:

1. The proposed equal rights constitutional amendment.
2. Reduced dependence on locally collected property taxes.
3. Establishment of a Department of Community Development.
4. Assurance of adequate child care services.

Each member of the task force was assigned the responsibility of "staffing out" a series of recommendations. In some cases, where recommendations had implications for several governmental functions, more than one institution was asked to provide an analysis and position paper. Participation by the "line" agencies, such as HEW or the Department of Labor, was to be solicited on a selective basis. HEW provided a full-scale analysis of its own of the commission's recommendations.[10]

The fact that this review exercise was proceeding within the Executive Office of the President was deliberately not made widely known. However, as is common in Washington, its existence became an open secret. John D. Rockefeller III, the former chairman of the commission, visited with Ed David and members of his staff in August 1972 to acknowledge and encourage the follow-up review. He took the occasion to point out the fact that the commission, rather than going out of business, was to simply undergo a transformation into a "Citizen's Committee on Population and the

American Future." The commission members and staff had already feared the burial of their massive report by a less-than-enthusiastic political system and had taken pains to perpetuate and promote its findings.[11]

The Task Force met through the fall of 1972 and eventually developed a series of position papers for the thirty-two recommendations which called for federal action or attention. In November 1972, the task force invited Patrick Moynihan to meet with it and to contribute his thoughts on how the government should respond. In this, his views were candid and revealing. He observed that the fertility rate in the United States had dropped substantially since the presidential message in 1969. The public focus on a population "crisis" had abated or had transformed itself into other national concerns. Therefore, in his judgment, there was little positive need for any governmental response to the Population Commission's report and recommendations.

In January 1973, a report of the task force's review was sent to the President's staff. The covering memorandum revealed a good deal about the political overtones of this set of issues. The task force had recommended the release of a presidential statement on the Population Commission report. However, the chairman of the task force personally advised against this, arguing that "there appears little to be gained from such a statement. Indeed, it might simply reactivate the ardent advocates at a time when there is less general concern over the issue of U. S. population growth than there was in 1969."[12] The position proposed concerning the Population Commission's recommendations "welcoming and planning for population stabilization" was correspondingly revealing for its sensitivity to political concerns:

In the opinion of the task force, it seems premature and inadvisable for the Federal Government to endorse population stabilization as a national goal at this time. Population stabilization as a matter of public policy should be accorded a generation of discussion and debate. However, the data on the national birth rate indicate that the citizenry at large may have reached a decision on this issue, since fertility in the United States has dropped below the level necessary to achieve zero population growth, namely, 2.1 children per family. If the birth statistics reflect a national consensus, then no statement by the Federal Government is required. It should be noted that the evidence gathered by the Commission to indicate that population growth is on balance nationally detrimental is weak at best, and far from persuasive. There are political and sociological implications of population stabilization which require further study and analysis. Moreover, federal "planning" for population stabilization implies a direct federal role in influencing such factors as family size and patterns of marriage, and such a role is neither consistent with Administration policy nor supported by national consensus.[13]

7. SOME ADDITIONAL ISSUES

There were at least two additional exercises in which the presidential science advisory apparatus was deeply involved and whose descriptions further illuminate the relationships between scientist-adviser and the public policy machinery. One was a heroic but abortive attempt in 1970–71 to write the first of a series of annual reports on science and technology. The other was a totally politically motivated attempt to highlight certain selected federal governmental programs characterized by a high scientific or technical content under the title of "New Technology Opportunities." In both of these cases, there was a strong motivation to serve political desires. In both cases, science and technology were treated, not as ends in themselves but for their value in achieving national purposes. The practical and applied uses of technology and the utility of science as a progenitor of technology were the underlying themes. In both cases, the science advising apparatus pressed itself into service (or was impressed into service) in an attempt to be "useful" to the political machinery. In each case, the effort involved was prolonged (measured in months). Large numbers of scientists and engineers—both within and without the government—were engaged in the exercises. After a massive, prolonged, phrenetic, and painful effort in each case, the ultimate goals were not achieved. Each project was ended short of producing a final product.

An Annual Report on Science and Technology

Background. In the first approximation, the general concept of an annual report of the activities of almost any function of government sounds both elementary and innocuous. Real problems arise when a report attempts to step out in front of the safe and the ordinary—when it contains something of real substance which may provoke and inform.

Annual reports may serve a variety of purposes. Most are designed to take stock of the state of affairs for the area concerned. A large part of most documents is dedicated to informing the readership about the status of development or growth or evolution for the function discussed. Annual reports are often designed to serve frankly political purposes. The political purposes may not always be those of the party in power. As in the case of reports from the advisory councils to the NIH, for example, it is often the constituency for those agencies of government that is prominently served by annual reports. A third purpose for an annual report addressed to the Congress and to the President is an element of accountability. When the Congress requires (typically through legislation) that an agency or function of the executive branch furnish it with a (public) report on its activities, the legislature exacts a form of public accounting of certain of the agency's activities, accomplishments, expenditures and, at times, plans. This accounting, of course, establishes or solidifies lines of congressional jurisdiction over executive branch business and causes the executive to share material and ideas which could become important in the political bargaining among those sharing powers.

Toward the end of 1970, the science adviser and others persuaded the President and his staff that it would be to the political benefit of the President to provide a document which examined the contributions of science and technology to national needs. The report, which was considered to be the first of a continuing series, was frankly conceived of as a "political" document that would "treat science and technology in a policy, social and economic context."[1] It was not intended to review the state of the art for the several branches of science and engineering. It was, rather, conceived of as a vehicle for examining the contributions of science and technology to the achievement of national purposes and national goals and for determining additional opportunities for furthering these national interests. This was clearly a report that was to consider science, not for science's own sake, but as a necessary ingredient in achieving national desires—especially in domestic areas such as housing, transportation, health, or the environment.

In an important sense, the tenor of this report was to be an optimistic and forward-looking one—consistent with the major traditional threads of the nation. The viewpoint to be explored and developed in this report assumed that there *was* something important that science and technology had to offer to national well-being. At the same time, the report would put science and scientists on notice. The research and development enterprise, in the aggregate, represented a sizable national expenditure—much of it from public (governmental) sources. The combination of this expenditure, large enough to be visible and competitive with other claims on the same resources, and of the public expectations raised or implied by scientists over the years as to what science promised society, led to a demand for identifiable, practical results. With the results of the Apollo IX flight fresh in the public's mind, the question "since we went to the moon and returned, why can't we similarly produce similar technological solutions in behalf of decent housing, convenient transportation, cure of cancer, etc.?" became commonplace. Practical results for what were perceived of as major domestic problems were increasingly called for. This report was to explore what was possible and what should be expected. There were, in addition, some important trends already in place that were to influence both the topics discussed and the flavor of the discussion:

1. The military sponsorship of research performed in university-based departments and institutes had become imcreasingly controversial. The Department of Defense and the military services had underwritten research in academic settings for many years. Much of this was basic research which was thought to be of ultimate value in the design of military systems. However, an increasing number of voices were raised during the 1960s opposing the general concept of military support for scientific research performed in academic laboratories, especially for classified projects. Largely as a result of this viewpoint, the Congress decreed by statute that the Defense Department was prohibited from the sponsorship of scientific projects which were not clearly relevant to the missions of the military agencies. This legislation, known as the Mansfield amendment,[2] succeeded in reducing the totality of the military's research budget, in transferring some projects formerly of military sponsorship to civilian agencies, and in furthering the trend of shifting the emphasis of the government's research and development effort away from strategic towards domestic issues.

2. The combination of the growing fear of inflation plus the accumulated financial drain of the Vietnam War conspired to bring about constraints on government spending. Since R & D expenditures comprised about one-third of the total of "controllable" expenditures by the government, restrictions on the growth of science budgets of government agencies became prominent features.

3. About the same time, the budgetary process was subjected to some further constraints—dictated in part by an ideological viewpoint of the moment. It was argued, for example, that one of the tests for the appropriateness of federal support for research and development was the absence of any indication of private support. If a private economic sector required scientific

research for its own furtherance, that sector, it was argued, should provide those underpinnings, not the public till. It was only where the forces of the private market were absent or failed that the government should shoulder a responsibility.

4. In a complementary fashion, there developed a general government policy stance opposing the support of training (including the training of scientists). Since the underwriting of the training of scientists had been a traditional role for the government, a new moratorium on training support caused vocal opposition. However, the administration's own position was popularly supported by the public's impression at that time of a relative surplus of scientists and engineers.

5. The national space program was under serious review even as it was delivering its ultimate product. The national space effort had been recognized by some early in its planning as unusual since it would start to be put out of business before its final product was completed.[3] However, none had taken this early admonition very seriously. Further, in the promotion of the program, numerous public expectations had been raised of the tangible benefits to the solution of civilian domestic problems from the space program. In the sense of a technological gadget in search of a mission, an enormous amount of effort had been applied to realize these byproduct benefits of the space program with only very limited success. For these reasons and others, the future of the national space program was under critical review.

6. There had already developed a broad national questioning of the proper role of science and, to a greater extent, technology in national life. Numerous thoughtful spokesmen pointed to the fact that the very successes of science and technology had transformed the relationships among men in ways that were not always foreseen or thought universally desirable. A questioning of science and technology—even an antitechnology attitude—had already begun to color in many ways the public discussion of national priorities.

7. There was already in place in the White House a review exercise which in a sense, was a different but complementary cut of the same material. A National Goals Research Staff had been established early in the administration, not to recommend goals for the nation but to discuss and explore major national aspirations and problems. Indeed, science and technology were a part of that discussion and, again as they served national intentions, were included in the discussion of the final report.[4]

Development of the Report. The process of developing the report constituted a massive effort. Those primarily responsible for early drafts of substantive chapters were professional members of the staff of the Office of

Science and Technology. In specific cases, additional assistance was sought from certain of the government agencies. In others, experts outside the governmental structure were asked to develop ideas and materials. The introductory and summary chapters were reserved for special handling.

An enormous cast of persons—writers, critics, and reviewers—was ultimately assembled to produce this opus. The draft report itself was correspondingly ambitious. The review draft contained twenty-four chapters of which the majority dealt with major domestic sectors and issues. Examples were agriculture, population, transportation, environmental quality, food, education, housing, and health. A single chapter was devoted to national defense. Seven chapters were set aside for issues or areas which transcended several sectors. Among these were discussions of energy, social sciences, and communication.

There were several important and reasonably consistent themes which pervaded this work:

1. Science and technology did have a useful and serious contribution to make to major domestic challenges. One of the goals of the government's science policy was to "promote the systematic and technological capabilities to clearly defined goals."[5] The historical pattern established for agriculture of translating efficiently and deliberately the products of scientific investigation into practical application was a lesson to be followed in other sectors. The report said this at many points:

The most powerful force shaping federal science policy for the coming years is the policy decision to reallocate the employment of our national resources in the direction of meeting the country's domestic problems—mainly in health sciences, education, the environment and urban improvement.[6]

2. To achieve this, according to the report, required a healthy partnership among government, the universities, and industry that "respects their independence and builds on their mutual interests."*[7] The major theme of this report, in brief, was highly pragmatic and was oriented toward how to harness science for its social sake, and how science, when properly utilized, could help in redefining or even identifying new national goals and possibilities.

The report included in many ways and in many places purely political

*It is interesting and ironic to note that a similar philosophic position favoring mission-related research and dedicated efforts to apply the fruits of science to national problems was beginning to emerge in Great Britain at about the same time. What became known ultimately as the "customer-contractor relationship" governing the support of science was the product of an extensive study by the Rothschild Commission in 1971. *A Framework for Government Research and Development* (London: Her Majesty's Stationery Office, November 1971). The "Rothschild Commission."

references–favorable allusions to policies and programs of the incumbent administration and critical appraisals of predecessor governments. For example:

In the 1960's, the directions of science policy did not give the impression of coherence and internal consistency. They served to emphasize policies for science and technology uncoupled from the use of science and technology in carrying out broader policies that actually affect the individual in our society.[8]

and:

Toward the end of the 1960's, it became apparent that there were emerging imbalances between the support and utilization of science and technology.[9]

Destiny of the Report on Science and Technology. The ultimate fate of this massive work, which in the end filled nearly 450 typewritten pages, represents an interesting lesson. Numerous, seemingly endless drafts of the chapters were written. Critical reviews were solicited from key persons within relevant government agencies and from experts in university or industry settings. Members of the President's Science Advisory Committee were assigned chapters for careful review. At one point, a professional writer-editor was engaged to forge some coherence among the written styles used in the several drafted parts.

This entire process consumed ultimately close to a year of constant attention. Yet, in the end, the report was not published. The reasons for this failure are interesting as they once again illustrate the difficult interreaction between advice on science and engineering specifically in behalf of the political process. This case is particularly interesting since the science advisory apparatus had striven conscientiously to produce a creditable analytic document that would be "useful" to the political machinery.

The report failed essentially because it proved impossible to satisfy two desires at the same time. When the report dealt frankly and in any depth with matters of real substance and real scientific importance, it inevitably touched on matters that were threatening and too hot to handle for the political operatives. When the report stepped back from its goal of having anything of real substance to say about scientific and technical contributions to an issue, the resulting text was inevitably bland and had nothing new to contribute. A discussion of the coupling of technology to improvements in the housing industry, for example, was seen as limited not by technology itself but by other barriers. A similar conclusion was reached in the case of transportation. To lift up and elaborate on these barriers to the coupling of science and technology to these sectors threatened to raise a whole series of difficult political problems at various levels of society.

In the case of population and family planning, the articulation of the government's policy toward limitation of family size and, specifically, toward abortion was a problem. Further, when examined carefully, the government's R & D program, put in place as a result of a presidential initiative on the population question, was found to contain elements which did not please the major industrial sector, traditionally responsible for contraceptive development and manufacturing.

Finally, the report, because of its nature and because of its comprehensiveness, effectively highlighted certain national goals. It did this most forthrightly in the form of a series of twelve "important assumptions about the evolution of society."[10] Throughout the substantive chapters on health and energy, etc., certain national goals were assumed or even made explicit.

As a result, the project designed to develop an annual report on science and technology fell of its own weight in 1971. Nothing more was ever heard of this concept until the Congress itself imposed such a burden on the Science Adviser in 1976 when it established the Office of Science and Technology Policy by statute. Among the statutory functions of the science adviser was an annual report. In view of this history, it is perhaps not surprising that the science adviser took special pains to pass on that particular responsibility to one of the government agencies, the National Science Foundation. Further, one should not be surprised that the version of that report ultimately published was nearly devoid of any content or substance.[11]

The New Technology Opportunities Program

A second, even more massive program was mounted by the White House to link technological resources to national needs. This second program, which ironically was begun at about the same time that the annual report concept was fading, was entirely the conception of the politically minded staff of the White House. In July 1971, John Ehrlichman, then assistant to the President for domestic affairs, called for the cooperation of nearly all of the cabinet secretaries plus the heads of certain other executive branch agencies, in mounting a study to determine opportunities for directing extra attention and money to areas of technology in behalf of selected national problems.[12] The stated objectives were to identify technological areas or ideas whose further development or refinement could stimulate innovation in the civilian manufactoring sector, bring about improvement in one or more domestic problem areas (health, housing, energy, etc.) and, perhaps, lead to an increase in employment. An interim report for the President was called for by September and a final report was due in November. Edward David, the science adviser, was given the responsibility of chairing the committee established to make the study.[13] The items and ideas ultimately selected were to be characterized as "bold, imaginative," and "innovative." The timing of this exercise was clearly not unrelated to the upcoming presidential election season.

This initial study was eventually to become one part of a large, centrally directed effort to sweep into a single, identifiable pile all the technologically oriented ideas that could possibly be related to recognized, political purposes. In September, the White House chose William Magruder, a former test pilot and chief of the President's ill-fated program to promote the supersonic transport, to manage the Technology Opportunities exercise.

Ultimately, over three hundred persons were involved. A management superstructure was put in place to sift and analyze the many ideas collected. Agencies were directed to develop proposals, together with estimates of what their cost would be and what their impact or benefit to national challenges would be. The entire process took on the distinct aura of a strict military exercise performed according to schedules, PERT charts, and cookbooklike criteria.[14]

The ideas developed or sent forward by the agencies for consideration as "initiatives" represented an enormous spread varying widely in quality and in newness. In many cases, the agencies (and sometimes their outside constituencies who saw a new opportunity for federal funds) offered old pet ideas warmed over or recast in new clothing to appear as "bold initiatives." All of the potential initiatives were placed in one of ten categories: employment; health care; environment; education; law enforcement; urban transit; conservation; community development; productivity; and trade. In each case, the technology initiative was submitted to an elaborate (although not necessarily accurate) system in which costs to the government were estimated and the political importance was gauged. In these latter terms, the "impact" and importance of each of the projects were estimated by members of the White House and the Executive Office and by groups of outside advisers called together as "Blue Ribbon Panels." In addition, a "political priority list" was determined by questioning selected members of Congress as well as members of the White House staff.

Over fifty projects or "technological opportunities" survived the screening process and were presented to the President in December 1971 in the form of elaborate background papers, "packaged" for political use. The President approved the interim product. The remaining time was to be spent in further refinement of the list, in determining how many of the projects, started by the federal government, could be eventually transferred to private sector ownership and responsibility, and in determining how best to display this total program as a series of "Presidential" initiatives.

In fact, however, this program too fell of its own weight. The closer scrutiny of these programs over the next several weeks betrayed a pronounced pattern of force-fitting of ideas into politically attractive categories with little careful consideration to the technical or programmatic quality of the ideas. All of this had been accomplished in a relatively indiscriminate fashion over a short period of time. The result was correspondingly thin.

Ultimately, a few of the projects that had been reviewed under this unusual umbrella survived to gain special budgetary attention. An augmented program in behalf of emergency medical care, a research program designed to relate emissions of air pollutants to ambient air quality, and a housing voucher experiment were examples. However, it became evident eventually that there simply was not sufficient worthy and valid material from all of this effort to be held up as a "Technology Opportunities Program." Eventually, all plans to advertise this program as a politically attractive "Presidential initiative" were dropped. It would be difficult at this writing to identify any area where technology has been usefully harnessed in behalf of national need as a result of this effort.

The principal lesson from this exercise is that the fundamental premises behind the Technology Opportunities Program were simply wrong or misguided. To conjure up on the spot a flashy, visible program of technologically based components designed nominally to meet national challenges simply could not be a serious effort. The superficiality of the thinking behind what was essentially a public relations effort was bound to lead to failure in the end. The very fact that this New Technology Opportunities Program came into being and was put under special management illustrated again the kind of frustration experienced by politicians with the careful, deliberate, and analytic processes which characterize science and scientists.

8. SUMMING UP

There has been an evolution in character of the scientific advisory machinery in the Office of the President. It has been led in directions that were not considered by its early scientific advocates and practitioners. However, the ultimate relationship between scientists and professionals and the public policy apparatus perhaps has still not clearly been defined. In latter years, from the scientists' side, there has been a steadily increasing attempt toward proximity to politics and toward useful articulation with the political machinery. From the politicians' point of view, the desire for scientific and technical counsel is not as compelling, and is inevitably tempered by political liabilities.

The early relationships between scientists and the White House were generally ones marked by modest and hesitating advice on strictly technical issues. The periods of advice were characteristically discrete and limited to specific questions. Scientists were generally fearful of too close an approximation to the political system and to politicians. Periods of substantial and sustained collaboration were unusual and were marked principally by the recognized importance to the nation of the successful pursuit of specific national projects or goals. The notable marriage between universities and government in behalf of agriculture remains perhaps the most outstanding example of cooperation—a concept born not of the imagination of the scientific and academic community but of politicians. The other area of successful collaboration was in time of war—especially during World War II.

The period since World War II might well be described as one in which scientists have been trying to find out *if* and *how* they can be useful to politicians and to the public policy machinery. Increasingly, members of the scientific and professional community have endeavored to prove their utility alongside others *at court*. All of this has been done, however, not without some ambivalence. Scientists in the service of the President still do not wish to compromise their ties to their own fraternity—especially those ties to academic settings.

The Reorganization Plan of 1962,[1] which "institutionalized" the science advisory apparatus, transferred to the White House office a number of functions which had nominally been the responsibility of the National Science Foundation. Part of the momentum for that transfer in fact had been the observation that the scientific leadership of the NSF had been highly conservative and not at all aggressive in being of assistance to the political processes. The mandate of science for policy making had simply not been fulfilled. The elevation of those functions to an office deliberately dedicated to the purpose was intended (at least by some) to facilitate and encourage a useful articulation between scientists and politicians on issues of major national importance.

The success, however, remained limited. As discussed above, Jerome Wiesner's influence in defense and national security areas was sharply delimited by the then National Security Adviser. A new set of territories covering a range of domestic issues was made the agenda for the Office of Science and Technology. However, the articulation remained anything but crisp.

The general issue of what the character of the interaction should be was raised anew in the period 1974-76. The functions of the President's Science Adviser had been transferred, in part, back to the director of the National Science Foundation. After a period of essentially no response to that move from scientists and academicians, a number of spokesmen began to consider what presidential science advisers realistically could be expected to accomplish.[2]

Most important, perhaps, the 1974 report from the National Academy of Sciences on "Science and Technology in Presidential Policy-making" was designed explicitly to persuade those in the political process that scientists *did* have something useful to contribute to the public policy machinery![3] (Note the sharp contrast between the spirit expressed by this report and that represented by the National Academy of Sciences in the 1930s, when President Roosevelt was seeking pragmatic answers to the depression.) Major recommendations and conclusions in the 1974 NAS report are revealing in this regard:

. . . make explicit the relationship between the science and the technology advisory mechanism and the other areas of the White House and the Executive Office. . . .

. . . extend the services of the mechanism more deeply into civil problems while restoring those of national security.

. . . recognize two functions that need improvement in the Executive Office of the President in relation to that of providing independent scientific and technical counsel, *viz.*, the study of policy options in a planning context and upgrading analytical and technical capability for dealing with day-to-day decisions in the Executive Office.[4]

For a limited period, the Congress gave nominal support to this same spirit. During the period 1974-76, a number of legislative proposals were considered to give the presidential science advisory mechanism a statutory basis. A prominent proposal on the Senate side contained a provision which called on the science advisory mechanism to provide "scientific and technological analysis and judgment for the President with respect to major policies [and] plans" and to "define a coherent approach for applying science and technology to critical and emerging national problems."[5]

How should we assess the results of the presidential science advisory apparatus, especially in behalf of domestic issues during the first half of the 1970s? According to the advocates of the position that presidential advisers do have a substantial role, one would like to measure these results, perhaps, in terms of tangible influence on policies and programs. Alternatively, one would be interested in determining the degree to which policy and program choices were better informed, their broad implications were understood, and their long-range implications were analyzed and assessed. A stock taking of the examples cited in this book from the domestic areas of health and the environment (which in my view are similar to the experiences for other domestic sectors) reveals a limited contribution to the public policy machinery.

For issues concerning the environment, a major political issue of the early 1970s, the Office of Science and Technology participated in deliberations on legislation and design of programs to assure clean air and water. However, in the face of overwhelming political attractiveness and popularity for the environmental movement, the science adviser had limited effectiveness in keeping the political strategies for clean air and water scientifically honest. There were instances where the science adviser's office attempted to step out in front of a political issue (regulation of environmental chemicals and pharmaceutical products in order to protect human health) and to deal with it forthrightly and analytically. Such instances, while useful to individual government agencies, were at times ignored by the remainder of the President's staff since they were ahead of their time. The study, *Chemicals and Health*, was an extensive, deliberate and highly analytical attempt to deal with the breadth of issues—economic, administrative, and legal, as well as biological—concerned with regulation of chemical substances. Regulatory reform, destined to become of political importance, was still two to four years from its full flowering and, hence, this study was of limited usefulness to a President in 1972 and 1973.

The science adviser's office did play a clear and highly useful role in behalf of a number of specific regulatory decisions. The list of those which reached the White House office was a long one. From the science adviser's point of view, the common challenge among all of these was to assure that the scientific basis for the decisions was valid. From the viewpoint of the majority of the White House, the usefulness of the Science Adviser's role was to defuse any controversy which these decisions might bring with them.

In a few instances, the President's office clearly attempted to use his science adviser to further his political ends. These instances characteristically provoked substantial anxiety and ambivalence from the science adviser and from his staff. Perhaps one of the best illustrations was the request by the President to explore and assist in the establishment of the Quality of Life Review Process. The inherent difficulties in pursuing the President's political desires in this case were enormous and serve to illustrate the limitations in the marriage between Presidents and their science advisers.

For population and family planning (as for essentially all scientifically related national programs and policy areas), the science adviser's office played an ongoing role in advising on the budget and on certain administrative matters. The science adviser did add his voice to that of others within senior positions in the government in urging that the population question was worthy of presidential attention. His office did have a hand (along with others) in designing the political strategy for population and family planning (although the leadership for that function was assumed by one of the other presidential counsellors). Perhaps the most significant role served by the science adviser's office in behalf of population affairs related to the review of the conclusions and recommendations of the Commission on Population Growth and the American Future. The science adviser did assume a "lead" role. Again, the task was clearly one of aiding the fortunes of the political machinery. By the time of publication of the commission's report the fertility rate had decreased and the political gain from further identification with the domestic population issue had largely disappeared. Several of the recommendations had already been implemented in one way or another. The task then was one of *disposing* of the remaining recommendations rather than accommodating them. From the political point of view, this was an eminently successful exercise. The science adviser's usefulness to the political process was substantial.

The Science Adviser's office did have a useful, early role in helping to design a political strategy for health. Again, this was done in the company of other contributors to the same subject in the ad hoc forum of the Health Policy Review Group. The product of this review was highly influential and became the centerpiece of the administration's National Strategy for Health. This exercise was somewhat unusual. It arose in great part because of the failure of the cabinet department to furnish a suitable program for the President. As a result of its contingent character, it was a short-lived exercise and the members of the original strategy planning group were not called upon under that title for any follow-up.

Most important from the science adviser's point of view, the most scientifically defensible position toward a national strategy for health was too far ahead of its time to be politically attractive. The proposal in 1970 of the science adviser to consider forthrightly the question of the major contributors to ill-health and to highlight the divergence between health status and the rising national expenditures for health was not embraced at that time. It was not immediately clear how to accommodate such a concept through political means. It tended to go against the traditional or common wisdom. Further, to follow such a concept very far carried with it the potential of additional political liabilities (reduction in cigarette smoking and infringement on the public's "right" to injure themselves with the combination of alcohol and driving). The Canadians, Australia, and several Western European nations did take up this issue in a forthright political manner, but only after another three to four years had passed.

Among the cases discussed in this book, the examples of successful interaction between the science advisory mechanism and the political machinery were generally those of short-term problems. In many cases they were frank contingencies where the political machinery was required to furnish a response in a very short period of time. The task, in many instances, was to determine how best to defuse or deflect politically troublesome issues. Except as general background, there was only very limited opportunity for applying the principles of deliberate, careful long-range projection or assessment. The political process is highly pragmatic and opportunistic. Timing is exceedingly important and generally does not permit the luxury of careful, long-range thought and analysis. Attempts by the science adviser to pursue such a course were generally treated as academic and not useful by the politically minded White House staff. In some instances, such attempts were seen as harmful politically —thus adding to the forces of rejection. There is in this, of course, a paradox.

Planning is something as a nation we cannot afford to do without. Yet, in practice, it is an institution we cannot afford to sustain politically. The major problem is not the technical hurdle of assessment or of predicting futures. Rather, the challenge, above all, is to make the products of analysis and forecasting politically palatable. The experience to date shows that as the processes of systematic analysis and prediction become better and better, they become correspondingly less and less politically attractive. The principal question raised concerning a science advisory mechanism in the White House is that of how large programs and policy decisions in the domestic arena are to be sorted out and to what extent can any administration afford the tools of systematic analysis and assessment.

It is interesting to note that other parts of the Western industrialized world are taking this question very seriously (although the pattern of accommodation is by no means a common one). The need for special assessment of public policies and public programs (including those which have technological elements) is very evident in various parts of Europe.

The Organization for Economic Cooperation and Development has begun an inquiry into the process by which government policies are formulated and carried out in industrialized nations. This inquiry includes an evaluation of the existing governmental structures for planning. At the heart of this inquiry is the seeming conflict between the traditional patterns of political negotiation or bargaining (especially in the more open of the democratic governments) and the felt need to analyze and plan ahead. The secretariat's background paper for this inquiry admits of this conflict:

Future studies may . . . implicitly question established views and practices and act as a catalyst to evolving the new concepts and policies required to tackle the changing problems such as inflation, for example, of modern industrialized societies. They may therefore have major political repercussions where they result in radically different perspectives from those held by the government. Where they are carried out with the government itself they may therefore be stifled, and for this reason a government may choose to encourage independent, critical planning activities in universities or elsewhere as a necessary, though perhaps painful means of improving the quality of policy-making.[6]

At this writing, a measurable number of industrialized countries have developed operating institutional devices designed to aid the processes of policy making through systematic planning and analysis. The Netherlands, in 1973, established the Scientific Council for Government Policy. A Secretariat for Future Studies was established in the Cabinet Office in Sweden in 1973. This group is less concerned with assessment of current government policies and more preoccupied with a period of time in the future beyond the concern of most of the administration. Nevertheless, the secretariat has access to top-level decision makers and is close to the process of government. The Central Policy Review Staff was established in Great Britain in 1970 to serve the cabinet and the government as a whole with analytic and planning activities for programs and policies. Importantly, the staff's products and advice to the government are almost always given confidentially.

The Prime Minister of Canada and his president of the Treasury Board in 1970 advanced the notion of small, policy-oriented ministries of state designed to engage in policy planning aimed toward a more "rational" process of government. It was reasoned that by marshaling information and the products of research and by fostering the use of certain analytic tools, the government could replace or at least balance the traditional sources of bargained or brokered power in cabinet affairs. In brief, it was assumed that the acquisition and organization of knowledge were synonymous with political power. (The enabling legislation was weakened somewhat through compromise during its passage precisely because it represented a threat to the traditional distribution of political power.)

Two ministries of state were established in 1971—one for urban affairs and the other for science and technology.[7] The choice of the latter reflected a strong faith in the tools of scientific planning (systems analysis) in aiding governing policy making. It also reflected an intense debate that had been going on over a science advisory mechanism.[8] The ministry (which has no operating functions) is designed to assist the prime minister and the Treasury Board in policy-making and program decisions.

Interestingly, as the ministry is conceived, great effort has been taken to separate the science advocate role from the advice-for-policy-making role. The academic scientific community has not been aggressively brought into the chambers of the ministry, and the traditional and prestigious instrument for outside advice, the Science Council of Canada, has been moved a further distance from the prime minister and his Privy Council.*[9]

Success of this Canadian experiment is not yet clear. The ministry has had four different ministers since its inception in 1971. The articulation of policies and the coordination of activities across traditional government sectors remains difficult in the face of established lines of jurisdiction and power. Finally, the expectations of the usefulness and level of development of the tools of analysis have not been matched in practice. Nevertheless, a most recent review urges continued optimism.

*Perhaps in a way symptomatic of this alienation, the Science Council of Canada published a critical review of the Ministry of State for Science and Technology.

What possibly can be done? What is different about the present era which may make the achievement of practical solutions a reality? It may be that there has been some maturing of public attitudes. Public acceptance of meaningful planning by government itself necessarily means public acceptance of explicit statements of goals and, at times, uncomfortable or undesirable attributes of political action. The admonition of urgency has been applied so often it has surely lost its sense of importance. Yet, is it possible that such factors as complexity, transience, and falsely raised public expectations for policies of the past have truly made the present era an urgent one for governments?

The late Nicholas Golovin of the Office of Science and Technology contemplated this subject in a manuscript some years ago, which, unfortunately, was not published before his death.[10] He concluded that:

American society urgently requires the invention of a new organizational mechanism to collect, interpret and analyze information, define potential problems and needs, develop pertinent alternative action plans . . . , systematically and in real time, evaluate the results of established programs, . . . and keep the government, the business community and the public . . . informed. . . .[11]

At the same time he noted the conflict:

A mechanism possessing the magnitude of resources and the continuity of life probably required by the scope, persistance and controversial nature of the issues with which it would be concerned—at any level of government—would not be accepted by the people generally and by the business community particularly as part of the existing branches of government. . . .[12]

Golovin foresaw the need to create a new institution which would possess the necessary analytic capabilities but in a way which would provoke a "minimum of disturbance to the existing balance of powers in the institutional structure."[13] Golovin's criteria for the new institutional arrangement were that it be located outside the existing governmental structure and that it be relatively powerless.

There is some question as to whether a relatively open, democratic government as we know it is compatible with the tasks proposed in this paper and performed within the government itself. The Office of Technology Assessment in the Congress is an attempt of just that sort. The proposals of the past few years for an Institute for Environmental Analysis[14] or for an Institute for Congress[15] reflect a view which favors the establishment of extragovernmental entities to assist from the outside the tasks of government planning and policy making.

Golovin judged that some analytic functions could be assisted by universities, ad hoc commissions, and other nongovernmental entities. However, he was convinced that to really do the job, a new, "fourth branch" of government termed by him an "Evaluative Branch" was necessary.[16] He saw this new entity, principally concerned with long-range issues, as purposely and necessarily divorced from the mainstream of government. It would provide the data, the analyses, and the alternatives that would "catalyze" the relations between the public, the business community, and the executive, legislative, and judicial branches.

I believe that Golovin was wrong for the right reasons. Unfortunately, there would be an uncertain patron for the output of the Evaluative Branch. There seems to be nothing that would guarantee that its output and advice would be anything but ignored if these appeared politically undesirable in the short term.

I agree with David Beckler when he says that the performance of the science advisory mechanism must be understood against the perspective or environment for White House decision making. I agree, too, with Beckler's contention that, in essentially any era, for any President, the forces of rejection are prominent. A science advisory function functions effectively only as long as the forces of rejection are suppressed.[17]

At the present writing, the prospects of engaging science advice and scientific methods for policy making within the executive branch of the government do not seem particularly favorable. The traditional incentives appear to militate against such an outcome, and the very nature of the political system seems to assure a continuation of that pattern of incentives. Emerging structures in governments of other industrialized nations are important to consider and should be studied carefully. Yet, one finds evidence of continued incompatibility of traditional functions of democratic government and those of rational analytic and anticipatory study for policy making. A recent commentary on the Central Policy Review Staff in Great Britain is revealing on this subject:

The Central Policy Review Staff (CPRS) is potentially the most important single innovation in the organization of British Government in recent times. At the same time, its long term survival is in doubt. . . . One great fear is that CPRS may eventually turn into a Prime Minister's Department which would increase his power relative to [that of the Civil Service departments] . . . . [18]

Moreover, the recent moves toward more openness in government, while undeniably desirable in their own right, can be expected to further exacerbate this dilemma. Those who point to the successes of the British Central Policy Research Staff and the Canadian Ministry of State for Science and Technology have placed great stress on the fact that these organizations do their business and offer their advice out of the public's view. The reasoning in this case turns simply around the desire to preserve the largest number of political opportunities and the greatest possible maneuvering room for the chief executive. This seeming conflict between orderly analysis and public access is a real one and has now been commented upon by others contemplating the science advisory apparatus.[19]

In my opinion, the challenge is a different one than is usually considered in discussions of this sort. The major tasks of analysis and study for policy making (and especially for "forward thinking") in domestic matters may well have to be performed not within but outside the structures of government. To the extent that this conclusion is a valid one, the implications for private institutional candidates for this task—universities, free-standing research groups, and the world of private philanthropy—are obviously very large.[20] Such a conclusion calls for the marshaling of the best intellectual resources into private or quasi-public aggregations created and dedicated precisely for the purpose.

However, the intellectual task is only half the challenge. The bringing of scholarly talent and imagination to bear on socially important issues through the performance of scientifically valid yet balanced and politically realistic studies is a necessary but insufficient ingredient. If one hopes to "nudge" the system by informing it, a great deal of careful attention must be devoted to *who* is to be informed and *how* the message is to be broadcast. That is, one must give careful thought to the real *client* for the information produced. In most discussions of this sort, the client is considered to be the government, itself—especially its executive and legislative branches. In fact, a broader, public client is a more appropriate one. If government is to be allowed the luxury of honest and full exploration of policy alternatives, there must be a different public view and attitude which would brook at times seemingly undesirable or unexpected choices for the public's future. That attitude does not seem to be at hand as of yet. It is therefore the job of provoking, of informing, and of raising the level of informed public debate which deserves our attention.

Admittedly, what is prescribed here may seem to be of a level of ambition and character quite alien to any who have trod this ground before. It is a task which a traditional, private philanthropic foundation or the trustees of a university would, on the surface, find quite outside their sphere of comfortable responsibility. Yet, in a modest way the process has already begun. The series of Energy Policy Studies of the Ford Foundation are certainly of this character.[21] In the case of every national issue of importance (and hence, marked by controversy), we will need a variety of "nudges"—of informative provocations—in order to create the kinds of informed political consensus necessary to stiffen the spine of the government and allow it to propose truly meaningful action for the benefit of future years.

In conclusion, it appears likely that we will need several organizations engaged in research for policy alternatives. This will raise severe challenges of public accountability and credibility, adequate and stable sources of funding, and freedom from political influence. I do not believe that we have yet discovered the appropriate vehicle for analysis (including science advice) for policy making, but the subject is too important to leave to conventional alternatives.

APPENDIX A. REPORT OF THE DOMESTIC COUNCIL HEALTH POLICY REVIEW GROUP

The Review Group, in the three weeks allotted for its work, has attempted to develop a coherent framework for policy decisions in the field of health.

Our report is intended to serve as the basis for a discussion of alternative health policies and program initiatives.

If agreement can be reached by Administration officials on the purposes of a National health policy and the appropriate Federal role, the choice among individual program proposals can proceed in a logical and consistent manner.

December 8, 1970   Final Copy

Part I: The State of American Health Care

Statements about a "crisis" in the provision of health services have reached almost epidemic proportions over the last decade. *Fortune Magazine* said in a recent feature article "American medicine, the pride of the Nation for many years, stands now on the brink of chaos."

What are the facts?

A. *What's Right with American Health Care?*

Indices of physical health show an improvement in the general health status:

—The average American life span has increased from 49.2 years in 1900 to 70.2 years in 1968.

—The number of disability days (per person, per year) has decreased from 16.3 days in 1961 to 15.3 days in 1968.

According to a variety of measures, the National effort to improve health has been increasing:

—National expenditures for health care have been growing faster than GNP.

While GNP has grown 72% since 1950, health care spending has increased 164%.
–The number of physicians has increased from 289,000 in 1963 to 338,000 in 1969, up 17%.
–Health insurance coverage has been extended from 72% of persons under 65 in 1962 to 78% in 1970.

These facts indicate that health status is improving and that the Nation has not been grossly negligent in resource development or financing. But there are serious problems.

B. *What's Wrong with American Health Care?*
   Major problems fall into three categories:
1. *Rising Medical Costs*
   –While the consumer price index rose from 103.1 in 1960 to 127.7 in 1969, the price index for medical care rose from 108.0 to 155.0–twice as fast.
2. *Disparities in Health Status*
   Gross statistics mask important subpopulation differentials.
   –*Race.*–Infant mortality in 1968 for whites was 19.2 deaths per thousand live births; for all others, 34.5 deaths per thousand live births.
   –*Income.*–Average disability days for families with $3,000 annual income is 22.8 per person, per year, compared to 13.8 days per person, per year, for families with $10,000 or more annual income.
   –*Occupation.*–Average disability days among those employed in the mining industry is 14 days per person, per year, compared to 11.4 days per person, per year, for all employed.
   –*Geography.*–Average disability days for farm families is 17.1 disability days per person, per year, compared to 15.0 for the metropolitan dweller.
   –*Sex.*–Women have an expected life span several years longer than men.
3. *Maldistribution and Improper Utilization of Health Care Resources*
   –37% of the Nation's counties have two-thirds fewer doctors on a per capita basis than the National average.
   –Recent research indicates that large numbers of unnecessary surgical procedures are performed each year.
   –Chances of successful recovery from the same surgical procedure performed in a teaching hospital are significantly greater than in a non-teaching hospital.

Part II: The Federal Role Today

Repeated statements of concern about the Nation's health care system have been met with more Federal programs, more Federal spending.

Unfortunately, the process has gone forward without benefit of a guiding policy framework.

A. *Types of Federal Intervention*

The Federal Government has attempted to intervene at virtually every point in the Nation's health care system.

It has sought to influence both the demand and supply of health services. *Demand* has been stimulated by major new financing programs (Medicare and Medicaid). Attempts have been made to stimulate *supply* through manpower training, construction, and research programs.

B. *Scope of the Current Federal Role*

Since 1960, Federal spending for health has risen from $3.5 billion to an estimated $21 billion in 1971.

In 1960, Federal spending for health comprised 13% of National health expenditures. In 1970, an estimated 27% of the total will be from Federal sources, a doubling in ten years.

The shift in responsibility away from the private sector to the Federal Government has been accompanied by a dramatic change in the *composition* of Federal spending.

TABLE I

Federal spending	1960	1971	Change
	$3.5 billion	*$21 billion*	
Biomedical research	14%	8%	−6%
Military and VA care	48%	15%	−33%
Health payments for Poor/Aged	13%	63%	+50%
All other	25%	14%	−11%
Total	100%	100%	

Part III: A National Health Policy for the 70's

The Health Review Group believes that the Administration should adopt a coherent set of principles as the basis for National health policy in 1971.

Recognizing the complexity of the subject, the limitations of agreed-upon measures of benefits, and the short time of our assignment, we do not intend this paper to be a definitive or necessarily final product.

But it is a beginning. And it builds on what the Administration has, by many of its actions, identified as the primary purpose and principles of Federal policy in the field of health.

A. *National Goals in Health*

The Review Group recommends the following principles to define the Nation's major goals in health:

One, that our first preference should be *prevention*, that is, avoiding the need for medical care. Most Federal programs over the last decade have assumed that health deficiencies are unavoidable. Massive investments have been made to provide more health care. To the extent possible, we should focus more energy on avoiding health problems and thereby lessen the demand for expensive health services.

Two, that when medical care is required, the Nation should be able to provide it on a basis which assures:

—*Equity*: that all citizens, regardless of their economic position, have available to them a reasonable and basic standard of medical care; and

—*Efficiency*: that we use our health care resources more efficiently in order to stem the recent and unacceptable rate of price inflation for health care services, including using new scientific and technological developments to increase the productivity of the health care industry.

B. *The Federal Role*

The Federal Government should play a leadership and catalytic role in health. It should take the lead in developing a framework for assigning responsibility (Federal, State, local, and private) and in developing and disseminating new ideas.

As far as direct action is concerned, the Federal Government's role should be to undertake those programs and activities which no other institution in our society can perform, or which we can perform so much better that Federal action is warranted.

In developing and carrying out health policies which meet this test, the Federal Government must make maximum use of its existing leverage, derived from the fact that we already expend one dollar for every three that is currently spent in the Nation's health care industry.

The Federal role can be implemented through four principal devices—taxing, spending, regulation, and moral suasion. When an activity has been determined to be totally or partially Federal, it should be evaluated to determine which of these devices will accomplish best the defined program purpose.

Our political challenge in 1971 will be to redirect the growing debate on National health insurance into a proper debate on the entire subject of National health and to demonstrate that those who are concerned only with financing are not dealing with the fundamental problem.

C. *Seven Major Decision Areas*

The sections which follow are based on the health policy principles and concepts of the Federal role outlined above. Although by no means a complete survey of available options, they include the key alternatives presently available for major decisions.

The seven areas are interrelated. The first six relate to improving the *supply and efficiency* of health care. The seventh is *Family Health Insurance*. (Our ability to start FHIP in fiscal 1973 or 1974 without grave price inflation will depend in large measure on our success in reforming the supply side of the equation in the next few years).

In reading all seven sections, it is important to keep in mind that they do not represent *finished programs*; they are discussions of basic strategic and policy alternatives. Once the general directions are determined, each will require careful development, cost-estimating and legislative specifications.

1. *New Approaches for Training Medical Manpower*
(a) *The Problem.*—The costs of medical education have soared in recent
  years. Many medical schools are running into big deficits. Increasingly,
  they are turning to the Federal Government for short-term emergency
  "bail out" grants that do not solve the basic problem or stabilize the
  base of support for medical education.

  There is general agreement that some increase in the output of medical manpower is needed, although the rate of increase is in dispute.
  This applies to physicians and allied health professionals alike.

  The present pattern of Federal assistance for medical education is
  erratic—relying on a mix of formula grants, student scholarships, and
  special purpose project grants—and shows no clear policy.

  Medical education needs reform—in its curriculum, its duration, its
  attentiveness to research and patient care, and its fiscal base.
(b) *The Federal Role.*—The Federal responsibility for medical manpower
  has several bases:
  (1) The Nation "values" health and doctors, and the public perceives
      the support of medical education as a Federal task.
  (2) Federal financing plans (e.g., Medicaid, Medicare) have sharply in-
      creased the demand for health care; there is some Federal obligation
      to respond to attendant pressures on *supply*, particularly of medical
      manpower.
  (3) Health care personnel move across State lines and are a National
      resource.
  (4) To the extent that medical schools are (or should be) engaged in
      health care and in reform of the delivery system, the Government
      has an interest in their activities.
At the same time, it must be noted that because physicians generally earn
high incomes, the Federal Government should be able to recoup part of its
investment in their education.
(c) *Options.*—The Review Group offers three alternative strategies to gov-
  ern Federal support of medical education. (Any two or all three approaches could be combined.) The emphasis here is on physicians;
  but the same fundamental options would guide our approach to other
  health personnel as well.
  (1) *Capitation Funding*: Under this approach medical schools would
      receive equal amounts per student enrolled. This is fundamentally a
      form of "first dollar funding" where schools would know in advance
      how much they would get from Washington. They would be respon-
      sible for finding the rest of their funds—their "last dollar" costs—
      themselves.

      Under this approach, various types of incentive bonuses should be
      added that would encourage curriculum reform, new types of
      teaching methods and institutions, and additional functions (e.g.,
      sponsorship of HMO's) for the medical schools.

      The advantages of this capitation-bonus funding approach are:
      —This is the most popular approach in the medical community and

and is advocated by the Carnegie Commission and Association of of American Medical Colleges, among others.

—It rewards "output" (number of students) and, if the amount per student is high enough, would encourage expansion.

—It is even handed, treats all schools equally, and would seem to be a rational, long-term basis for Federal assistance.

The disadvantages of the capitation-bonus approach are:

—It takes no account of different costs in various institutions: a major research center, for example, costs more than a "degree mill".

—It assumes no responsibility for the viability of the institutions themselves; some medical schools, for which the amount per student is insufficient, might close.

—The minimum per student rates ($2,000–4,000, per year) at which this plan would be politically viable make it an expensive program.

(2) *Student Aid*: This approach would channel the funds through individual students rather than institutions. It would be possible to use student loans as well as grants and thus recoup a larger share of the Federal investment; repayment might be based on actual earnings (e.g., pay back a percentage of income, rather than a fixed amount).

The advantages of the student aid approach are:

—It is consistent with the Administration's basic higher education policy.

—It could be set up in a way that takes account of student financial need and assigns to the taxpayer a smaller share of the cost of educating wealthy students.

—Although "forgiveness loans" to medical students have worked poorly in the past, with changes, this approach might provide leverage to distribute doctors to places where they are needed (e.g., forgive the loan to a doctor who practices in a low-income area or in a Health Maintenance Organization).

The disadvantages of the student aid approach are:

—It is unstable and unpredictable from the viewpoint of medical schools.

—It creates a tremendous burden of indebtedness for young doctors and might thereby encourage them to go into rich areas or lucrative specialties instead of where they are needed.

—It is politically not very attractive.

—It might discourage low-income students from entering medicine.

—Insofar as it depends on loans rather than grants, it is not a realistic way to finance allied health professionals.

(3) *Negotiated Contracts*: Under this approach, the Government would continue, as under current law, to provide backup funding to medical schools in financial distress. This is a form of "last dollar" funding, but, unlike the present approach, it would require the development of a total institutional plan by each medical school and the negotiation of a contract with the Federal Government to cover the deficit. Included in the contract would be considerations

of enrollment expansion, research, patient care, curriculum reform, etc.

The advantages of the negotiated contract approach are:

—It requires minimum dislocation of current laws and practices.

—It commits the Government to institutional stability.

—It provides incentives for reform, improved management and planning and careful cost accounting.

—It recognizes heterogeneity by forcing separate treatment of each institution.

The disadvantages of the negotiated contract approach are:

—It is extremely complex to administer.

—It involves the Federal Government deeply in the internal affairs of every medical school.

—It implies the redefinition of medical education as a "public utility" subject to Federal regulation and subsidy.

—It might reduce fiscal responsibility for medical education on the part of States, private sources and the students themselves.

—The actual dollar cost of ensuring the viability of every instituition might become quite high: it is an "open-ended" Federal program.

—This approach may not result in increased output.

(4) *Next Steps*: Needed for decision in this area are: (1) an analysis of the relative costs of any one or a combination of the reforms discussed above; specifically, the cost analysis should assess the offsets under existing programs (e.g., research, traineeships) that could result from a new approach, along with a detailed tabulation of the total costs of the new approaches at different levels of expenditure, enrollment and with varied objectives; and (2) a political and programmatic evaluation of how any given reform would affect the structure of medical education (particularly its high dependence on research) and thus how fast it could actually be put into place and with what consequences.

2. *Reform of the Medical Care Delivery System—Stimulating the Development of Health Maintenance Organizations (HMO's)*

(a) *The Problem.*—In addition to the production of medical manpower, there is an urgent need for organizational reform to use the Nation's medical manpower and other resources more *efficiently*.

The medical care system is poorly organized to deliver services at reasonable costs. Insurance pays for just about anything that is charged. Neither doctors nor patients have effective incentives to economize.

Beyond the method of payment, the medical system is not oriented to maintain health, but only to provide care once a health crisis has occurred. There are no financial incentives for providers to undertake health maintenance or preventive measures.

(b) *The Federal Role.*—In March of this year, the Administration proposed amendments to Medicaid and Medicare establishing *"Health Maintenance"* as a major basis of our strategy for improving the organization of the Nation's health care system.

Under these amendments, which have passed the House, we would foster the growth of "Health Maintenance Organizations" (HMO's) designed to guarantee their members the provision (not merely the financing) of a wide range of hospital and physician services in exchange for a fixed prepayment fee.

HMO care employs different incentives than the present system. The Health Maintenance Organization agrees upon a fixed per capita payment in advance and then takes responsibility for deciding what services the patient should receive and furnishing those services. By benefitting from "patient well days," not patient sickness, HMO's are motivated to prevent illness, and failing that, to promote prompt and thorough recovery through efficient delivery of services.

The HMO approach is well suited to the concept of trying to limit direct Federal intervention and using our leverage devices to the maximum. Basically, what is involved is a redirection of existing Medicaid and Medicare funds so that there is an incentive to purchase medical services on a prepaid contract basis, rather than piecemeal and after the fact.

(c) *Options.*—The Administration could propose a financial assistance program to stimulate the development of new HMO's. Organizations which could become HMO's would include existing medical clinics, public general hospitals, medical centers and their teaching hospitals, neighborhood health centers, and a variety of other organizations. The program could include the following major components:

(1) *A loan guarantee program.*—The risks involved in HMO development and the fact that this is a new venture in health suggests that a major loan guarantee program, for construction initial operating costs, would be appropriate. (Existing loan guarantee programs cover construction costs only). Loan guarantees use substantially less Federal funds than direct Federal loans or grants for a given investment level, and the discipline of having to go to the private capital market would help screen out programs which are unlikely to become financially viable within a reasonable period.

(2) *A direct loan program* could also be used to provide funds to *public* HMO's. These loans, intended to provide a substitute for the risk capital of private, profit-making organizations, would cover initial HMO costs during the two–three year period before an HMO becomes self-sustaining. These loans could be limited to HMO's in what are defined as health service scarcity or poverty areas.

(3) *A grant program* could be provided as well, to subsidize start-up costs and initial operating deficits of HMO's in selected underserved areas.

(d) *Next Steps:* The encouragement of HMO's could become a major objective of the Department of HEW. The Department should be asked to cost out in detail the various alternative approaches available. This analysis should include a projection of costs and numbers of new HMO's added over 10 years for each alternative—loan guarantees, direct loans and grants.

3. *Overcoming Legal Obstacles to Reform*
(a) *The Problem.*—There are two broad categories of legal obstacles to reforms that the Review Group (and most others concerned with this field) agree cause serious delivery system problems.
   (1) *Restrictions on group practice* exist in many States. These vary in kind, but their usual effect is to make it illegal or difficult for physicians to engage in group practice, or for insurance or medical institutions to sponsor Health Maintenance Organizations(HMO's).
   (2) *Restrictive health manpower licensing practices.* Laws which limit the practice of medicine via licensing or which define the functions that licensed personnel may perform also prevent the efficient use of health manpower in many States.
(b) *The Federal Role.*—Several considerations should be kept in mind in deciding upon the appropriate Federal approach to minimizing these problems:
   —The organization of health care and the use of health manpower are in a state of flux. Variety and experimentation are needed. The Administration should avoid freezing in a single approach.
   —Any action in these areas is an intrusion upon a traditional State function. The Constitutional, legislative, and judicial waters are uncharted as to where new types of Federal actions are warranted. And the political prospects of major action are uncertain.
   —The medical profession, however, including the American Medical Associations and the American Hospital Association, are agreed that reforms are needed.
   The Department of HEW, OEO, VA, and the Review Group are nevertheless agreed that any strategy should attempt to:
   —Remove barriers to group practice and other new forms of health organization and delivery, but without limiting the range of experimentation.
   —Reduce restrictive licensing practices and provide maximum flexibility for physicians, HMO's, hospitals and others to use physicians' assistants and other health sub-professionals.
   —Encourage the training, recruitment and deployment of physicians' assistants and other allied health personnel.
(c) *Options.*—There are three major alternative strategies which HEW could be asked to develop in more specific terms for inclusion in a 1971 health strategy.
   (1) Rely principally on "moral suasion" and other forms of leadership to urge States and private organizations to amend restrictive laws and effect other reforms. The principal hazard with such an approach, of course, is that it may have no effect.
   (2) Develop an array of "carrots and sticks" to push the States toward

changes. For example, make major health programs (e.g., Medicaid, Hill-Burton) available only to States that adopt specified kinds of reforms, such as eliminating prohibitions to group practice or the use of physicians' assistants under defined types of conditions. A similar approach would make new grants available to support experimental programs in these areas. This strategy would probably be more effective than Option (1), but it could make programs complicated to administer, and might seem to attach "irrelevant" conditions to basic health care programs.

(3) Arrogate to the Federal Government a substantially larger share of the basic law-making and licensing authority in this area, in effect, "preempting" the field. This might include Federal licensure of medical sub-professionals and of HMO's. This is likely to be the most direct and potentially effective route, but it would have many political and Constitutional risks.

4. *Geographic Distribution of Medical Care—Manpower and Facilities*

(a) *The Problem.*—Merely increasing the supply of doctors will not solve the problem of geographic maldistribution of medical resources. Currently, 37% of all U.S. counties have less than a third as many doctors per capita as the National average.

(b) *The Federal Role.*—The Federal Government has tried to influence the geographic distribution of medical care through a smorgasbord of programs. We provide direct Federal services to 415,000 American Indians; support 250 OEO and HEW health centers, mostly located in scarcity areas; and fund 131 health programs for migrant workers. The Hill-Burton program includes special incentives for the location of hospitals in rural areas, but construction of facilities in these areas has often failed to attract physicians. There is also statutory authority for forgiveness of loans for nurses and physicians who practice in shortage areas. (The program for medical students has not been successful, but it has been limited by the fact that the forgiveness is available only for practice in a rural poverty area. The program for nurses has been much more successful).

(c) *Options.*—If the Federal Government wants to go further in providing health care resources in scarcity and poverty areas, the Review Group would put forward two options, both of which would involve additional direct Federal spending.

(1) The first option is to establish "Health Education Centers" in scarcity areas which would be satellites of university-based medical schools. These centers would provide a base for patient care, clinical training for medical students and residents, and continuing education programs for health personnel. Specifically, the proposal would involve construction grants to assist in the conversion of non-teaching community facilities (HMO's, community hospitals, neighborhood health centers) into teaching facilities, together with incentive grants to university health and science schools to encourage them to sponsor such affiliated centers. These centers would be

located in selected rural and poverty areas which could tie into planning now underway within the Administration for a "National growth policy."

The proposal is similar to a recommendation in the recent medical education report of the Carnegie Commission. If we set as a first step 20 centers in fiscal year 1972, the cost would be $40 million.

(2) The second option for improving the geographic distribution of health resources relates to the section above on Health Maintenance Organization (HMO's). Specifically, HEW proposes that financial incentives be provided to encourage the development of HMO's in scarcity areas.

(d) *Health Service Corps.*—An issue related to the geographic distribution of health resources is the pending legislation for a National Health Service Corps, which would provide two-year Federal personnel on a voluntary basis to deliver health services in scarcity areas. The bill passed the Senate 66–0 and is likely to be enrolled this year.

Reasons for signing it are: (1) that it would help serve poverty and scarcity areas; and (2) that it would capitalize on the social motivation of many young health professionals.

Reasons against are: (1) that it puts the Federal Government in the business of providing care directly; (2) that it contains a draft exemption, contrary to our policy; and (3) that it looks to be a typical "Great Society" approach with high drama, low dollars, and little assurance that it will work.

5. *Disease Prevention through Research and Education—Financed by an Increased Tobacco Tax*

(a) *The Federal Role.*—Disease prevention through research and education is of high priority, both for itself and as a means of reducing the pressure of demand on health care resources and prices. These activities are not provided in sufficient amount in the private market and require collective action, thus a clearly appropriate area for governmental action (and because of economic "spill-overs" and economies of scale), particularly Federal Government action.

(b) *Option.*—Secretary Richardson has proposed an increase in the Federal excise tax on cigarettes sufficient to raise the retail price by 20% (the tax is now 8 cents per pack) to finance health research and education activities, such as:

    —Cancer and other disease research;

    —Expanded citizen education on health including the effects of smoking; and

    —Aid for delivery system reforms and the training of medical manpower.

The Secretary's proposal states:

"Through a measured increase in the excise tax now imposed on cigarettes, we propose to promote the public health by encouraging a reduction in cigarettes consumption within the United States.

The reduction will be of a size that will neither (a) impose sudden, drastically adverse economic effects on farmers, factory workers, or the tobacco industry, or (b) encourage widespread public evasion."

Such a tax would yield $860 million and HEW estimates would produce 13.5 billion hours of life gained per year.

If a decision is made to pursue this initiative seriously, it should be discussed with the Department of Agriculture. (HEW's proposal envisions that a portion of the added revenues would be used for training and relocation assistance to compensate for anticipated tobacco industry losses.)

Arguments in favor of the increased cigarette tax are:

(1) The proposal could save 13.5 billion hours of life per year, materially reduce the extent of disability from ailments associated with smoking, and effect reductions in the demand for health care services.

(2) The proposal appears to be the only one to reduce smoking for which there is both the statistical support of effectiveness and a reasonable possibility of congressional acceptance.

(3) There is some precedent for linking a preventive device with a revenue raising device, e.g., the Administration's proposed tax on polluters and leaded gas.

(4) It would generate revenues to cover many of the possible health initiatives in this paper. We would be setting an example of financing our proposals and could argue that any Congressman who wanted to outbid us would likewise have to show his source of revenue.

Arguments against the increased tax are:

(1) Excise taxes are regressive, bearing most heavily on the poor.

(2) The "elasticity" of cigarette demand may not operate effectively on persons whose income is such that the additional cost is of no consequence.

(3) Reduction of cigarette consumption will have an adverse effect on farm families, the cigarette industry workers, the cigarette companies, and two States.

(4) During the last decade, while Federal cigarette tax receipts have increased by less than 10 percent, State tax receipts have more than doubled. The smoking deterrence purposes of the proposal are, therefore, being accomplished by the States. Moreover, because of the economic effects of excise taxes, an increase in the Federal excise tax on cigarettes may impede future State increases, and thereby deprive States of needed revenues.

6. *Oversight Body for Health Research*

(a) *The Problem.*—The Federal Government currently spends $1.6 billion on research that is related to health and medical care. This ranges from fundamental studies in theoretical chemistry sponsored by the National Science Foundation to very practical experiments in applied health care supported by NIH. Yet this vast research enterprise has never had a

coherent policy or a body to guide it. Particularly in an era of tight budgets, it is important to ensure the optimal use of Federal funds in this field.
(b) *The Federal Role.*—The Federal Government provides 60% of all funds spent in the U.S. for health research. Health research funds are spent principally in medical schools, unversities, and other non-profit institutions. There is a strong National interest in the annihilation of cancer, heart disease and other dread killers, as well as in combatting tooth decay and the common cold. The support of biomedical research is an appropriate Federal function because the benefits accrue to all the people.
(c) The President could establish a broadly-based Health Research Policy Advisory Committee, consisting of outstanding researchers, scientists, and physicians in the Federal employ and from universities and the private sector, as well as economists and public administrators experienced with the relationship between program expenditures and results in the public sector.

The purpose of the Committee would be to advise the President, perhaps through the Director of OMB and the President's Science Advisor, and the agency heads most directly concerned (HEW, NSF, OEO, DOD) on the direction of Federal policy in health research and on the optimal use of available funds. The Committee could at the same time serve as a "board of overseers" for the key health research agencies—NIH, NIMH, NSF, and VA.

The biggest drawback to this proposal is that the Committee could become an "advocacy group" pleading for more money, or be so abstractly scientific as not to be helpful to policy makers.

However, assuming that these tendencies can be curbed, this proposal has the advantages of: (1) being a bold step to give direction to powerful Federal agencies now conducting biomedical research; (2) having a low (or no) budget impact; and (3) giving the Administration an opportunity to highlight health research innovations in fields such as cancer, heart, and others.

7. *Family Health Insurance*
(a) *The Federal Role.*—Consistent with FAP and the Administration's "income strategy", the President on June 10, 1970 proposed to the Congress a Family Health Insurance Program (FHIP).

The President said legislation would be submitted at the beginning of the next Congress:
"to establish a Family Health Insurance Program for all poor families with children. This insurance would provide a comprehensive package of health services, including both hospital and outpatient care."
(b) *Relationship between FHIP and Health Services.*—A critical point about this Presidential initiative is that it must be linked with (and preceded by) efforts, such as those in sections (1) through (6) above to increase the supply of factors needed to provide health care (doctors, physicians' aides, health service institutions).

If FHIP goes into effect by fiscal year 1973, or fiscal year 1974, the acid test of health policy in 1971 is:

> *Can we increase the supply of health care services in the short-run so that this time a new financing system will not just be dissipated in higher prices?*

(c) *Elements of FHIP Plan Design.*—In designing a health financing scheme such as FHIP, there are six key variables. They are:

(1) *Cut-off level:* Up to what income level are families to be subsidized, e.g., $5,000, $8,000?

(2) *Scope:* What kind of services will be included, e.g., hospital only, physician services, dental care, eyeglasses?

(3) *Duration:* What limits, if any, will be placed on the services paid for, e.g., 14 days of hospital treatment, 12 outpatient visits, no limits?

(4) *Premium:* What regular contribution, if any, does the family covered make in advance to the scheme?

(5) *Deductibles:* At what stage does the family become entitled to benefits, e.g., after paying $100 out-of-pocket, after a family member is in the hospital one day?

(6) *Co-insurance:* Once benefits begin, what part of the bill, if any, does the family pay, e.g., none, 20%, 30%?

At any given level of total Government expenditure, if any of these variables is moved in the direction of expanding benefits, another must be moved to contract them. If more families are to be subsidized, then some families must get less subsidy. If more benefits are to be included, then some durational limit must be put on them, or the deductible increased, or the family's share of the payment (co-insurance) increased, or the premium increased.

(d) *The Cost of FHIP.*—When FHIP was announced, it was understood that it would absorb the cost of Medicaid in the year of its initiation.

At the November 10 meeting of the Domestic Council, Secretary Richardson made a proposal for FHIP which would include families up to $8000 income (part of the blue collar group), adding $3.0 billion to the Federal cost of Medicaid. (Present cost about $2.0 billion.) His proposal has been used as a basis for analysis in the sections which follow.

The Health Policy Review Group has established a FHIP cost-estimating Task Force under the direction of the CEA which will be available to analyze whatever alternative plan and cost combinations are felt to warrant further study.

(e) *Three Options.*—Below are three plans which demonstrate the range that can be obtained by possible combinations of the variables as listed in section (c) above. For purposes of illustration, each plan provides the same package of medical services (with an average value of $800 per family). Families with incomes under $3000 pay nothing at all, with the Federal subsidy decreasing gradually as income increases above $3000 in order to maintain the incentive to work. The gross Federal cost of each of the three programs is the same, $5 billion per annum ($3 billion more than Medicaid).

The major *difference* among the three plans is the extent to which a family pays for medical care through a fixed premium and the extent to which a family spends money when it actually receives medical care. The choice among the three plans depends in large part on how much the role of FHIP is to encourage low-income families to seek medical care and how much it is to protect families from the financial burden of large medical bills.

Option I – High Premium/No Price for Medical Care

Under this option, families would pay premiums on a sliding scale basis, paying more as income rises. They are then eligible to receive the specified set of medical services *at no additional cost*. By eliminating any charge for actually receiving medical care, this option puts primary emphasis on encouraging families to seek medical attention early in illness. Because its key characteristic is eliminating any charge for early medical care, less expensive programs using this approach must reduce coverage of the last dollars spent for medical care, leaving families exposed to catastrophic health expenses.

One disadvantage of this approach is that the high premium charged families in the upper income ranges may discourage them from joining the program.

Option II – No Premium/Higher Price for Care

Under this option, families would pay no premium or a very low premium, but instead pay a percent of their medical bills. There are two terms important to this plan which require definitions at this point in the discussion:

–the *deductible*, which is the portion of initial medical care charges which the family itself *fully* pays.

–*co-insurance*, which is the proportion of a family's medical care bills which it pays above the amount of the deductible.

Under this second option, there is no premium, but there are these two types of charges which families above $3,000 must pay; thus, in effect, introducing a "price" for medical care, which many experts believe is necessary to prevent overutilization of services.

According to the schedule of deductibles and co-insurance in the table on page 140, the co-insurance rate is higher for higher income families. Above the co-insurance range shown in the table, expenditures are reimbursed fully by the Government, thus taking care of catastrophic health expenses.

Discussion of Options I and II

Because under Option II families with income over $3,000 pay a price for medical care at time they receive it, they will tend to use less care than under Option I, where families obtain free care once they have paid the premium. As already noted, this is considered to be an advantage of Option II by those who fear that families will over-utilize medical care if it is free. It is considered to be a disadvantage by those who feel that lower and middle income families will not seek adequate preventive care if they must pay anything for it.

Our illustrative examples used in this report blur these basic differences in approach, since the package of medical services is the same in

Family income	What the family would pay				Value of insurance protection	Federal subsidy
	Premium	Deductible	Coinsurance rate	On charges between		
Option I						
$0-3,000	0	0	0	0	$800	$800
4,000	$200	0	0	0	800	600
6,000	500	0	0	0	800	300
8,000	800	0	0	0	800	0
Option II						
$0-3,000	0	0	0	0	800	800
4,000	0	$150	25%	$150-700	600	600
6,000	0	475	45%	475-1475	300	300
8,000	200	700	60%	700-2000	200	0
Option III						
$0-3,000	0	0	0	0	800	800
4,000	$150	$ 50	20%	$ 50-150	750	600
6,000	325	150	25%	150-450	625	300
8,000	500	250	30%	250-950	500	0

all plans. A more extreme example of Option I is a plan which limits hospital insurance coverage to say 14 days. A more extreme form of Option II is a plan with a high deductible, for example, a plan that only covers hospitalization in excess of 14 days.

Option III—Medium Premium/Medium Price

This approach is one of the many possible compromises between Options I and II. As shown in the table above, families would pay a premium which is lower than under Option I, and a higher percent of their medical bills, although a lower percent than under Option II. This plan, therefore, encourages families to use less medical care than does Option I, but more than Option II.

A variation which could be used in any plan is to define a deductible in terms of services rather than dollars. This enables the plan to discourage the use of some kinds of services without discouraging the use of others. A deductible of one hospital day rather than $75, for example, will discourage hospitalization but not routine physical examinations.

The Blue Collar Worker and FHIP.—The three options discussed here were developed with the objective of providing some help to blue collar workers. This is an important consideration which should be focused upon in the discussion of these three options and possible variants.

Part IV: Next Steps

Secretary Richardson in his memo to the President November 10 proposed a "sequence of events" on health in 1971 which would include:

(1) a section in the State-of-the-Union Message;

(2) a Presidential television address on health;

(3) a simultaneous detailed report on the Administration's health strategy ("Brandeis Brief");

(4) a Presidential message transmitting new legislation to the Congress; and

(5) a series of White House meetings in the spring and summer with health leaders.

If we are to make this kind of major effort, a number of steps are suggested which flow from this report.

As a first step, a decision should be made about the general approach for FHIP. Specifications and legislation should be drafted accordingly.

Second, contingency plans should be developed for combining FHIP with a re-introduced, and possible revised, Family Assistance Program (FAP) in the 92nd Congress. This bill could include other revisions of the Administration's "income strategy" approach to social policy besides FHIP.

Third, other possible Presidential health initiatives, along the lines contained in this report, could be developed and prepared for discussion by HEW, VA, OEO, DOD, and others. This report, prepared over a short period of time, could not fully cover all available decision options in health.

Fourth, if Presidential decision-items included in this report are determined to be desirable initiatives, work should be started to spell out legislative and administrative specifications.

Fifth, work should also be undertaken to develop in a full and detailed form an analysis of the Administration's achievements to date in health to be included in messages and reports next year. A similar effort should be undertaken as regards programs which we decide to reduce significantly or terminate, making the point that we have the will and clarity of purpose necessary to decide priorities and terminate programs that are not sufficiently important to be continued as part of the Administration's 1971 health strategy.

Members of the Health Policy Working Group

Dr. Edward J. Burger, Jr.
Office of Science and Technology

Mr. Lewis H. Butler
Department of Health, Education, and Welfare

Mr. Chester E. Finn, Jr.
White House

Dr. Irene Lurie
Council of Economic Advisers

Mr. Donald H. Murdoch
Office of Economic Opportunity

Mr. Robert E. Patricelli
Department of Health, Education, and Welfare

Dr. Benjamin B. Wells
Veterans Administration

Mr. John F. Evans
White House

Dr. Jesse L. Steinfeld
Department of Health, Education, and Welfare

Mr. Paul H. O'Neill
Office of Management and Budget

Dr. Richard P. Nathan, Chairman
Office of Management and Budget

APPENDIX B. THE WHITE HOUSE: PRESS
RELEASE, FEBRUARY 18, 1971

For release at 12 noon, est   *February 18, 1971*

Office of the White House Press Secretary

THE WHITE HOUSE

TO THE CONGRESS OF THE UNITED STATES:

In the last twelve months alone, America's medical bill went up eleven percent, from $63 to $70 billion. In the last *ten* years, it has climbed 170 percent, from the $26 billion level in 1960. Then we were spending 5.3 percent of our Gross National Product on health; today we devote almost 7% of our GNP to health expenditures.

This growing investment in health has been led by the Federal Government. In 1960, Washington spent $3.5 billion on medical needs—13 percent of the total. This year it will spend $21 billion—or about 30 percent of the nation's spending in this area.

But what are we getting for all this money?

For most Americans, the result of our expanded investment has been more medical care and care of higher quality. A profusion of impressive new techniques, powerful new drugs, and splendid new facilities has developed over the past decade. During that same time, there has been a six percent drop in the number of days each year that Americans are disabled. Clearly there is much that is *right* with American medicine.

But there is also much that is wrong.

One of the biggest problems is that fully 60 percent of the growth in medical expenditures in the last ten years has gone not for additional services but merely to meet price inflation. Since 1960, medical costs have gone up twice as fast as the cost of living. Hospital costs have risen five times as fast as other prices. For growing numbers of Americans, the cost of care is becoming prohibitive. And even those who can afford most care may find themselves impoverished by a catastrophic medical expenditure.

The shortcomings of our health care system are manifested in other ways as well. For some Americans—especially those who live in remote rural areas or in the inner city—care is simply not available. The quality of medicine varies widely with geography and income. Primary care physicians and outpatient facilities are in short supply in many areas and most of our people have trouble obtaining medical attention on short notice. Because we pay so little attention to preventing disease and treating it early, too many people get sick and need intensive treatment.

Our record, then, is not as good as it should be. Costs have skyrocketed but values have not kept pace. We are *investing more* of our nation's resources in the health of our people but we are *not* getting a full return on our investment.

BUILDING A NATIONAL HEALTH STRATEGY

Things do not have to be this way. We can change these conditions—indeed, we must change them if we are to fulfill our promise as a nation. Good health care should be readily available to all of our citizens.

It will not be easy for our nation to achieve this goal. It will be impossible to achieve it without a new sense of purpose and a new spirit of discipline. That is why I am calling today not only for new programs and not merely for more money but for something more—for a *new approach* which is equal to the complexity of our challenges. I am calling today for a new National Health Strategy that will marshall a variety of forces in a coordinated assault on a variety of problems.

This new strategy should be built on four basic principles.

1. *Assuring Equal Access.* Although the Federal Government should be viewed as only one of several partners in this reforming effort, it does bear a special responsibility to help all citizens achieve equal access to our health care system. Just as our National Government has moved to provide equal opportunity in areas such as education, employment and voting, so we must now work to expand the opportunity for all citizens to obtain a decent standard of medical care. We must do all we can to remove any racial, economic, social or geographic barriers which now prevent any of our citizens from obtaining adequate health protection. For without good health, no man can fully utilize his other opportunities.

2. *Balancing Supply and Demand.* It does little good, however, to increase the demand for care unless we also increase the supply. Helping more people pay for more care does little good unless more care is available. This axiom was ignored when Medicaid and Medicare were created—and the nation paid a high price for that error. The expectations of many beneficiaries were not met and a severe inflation in medical costs was compounded.

Rising demand should not be a source of anxiety in our country. It is, after all, a sign of our success in achieving equal opportunity, a measure of our effectiveness in reducing the barriers to care. But since the Federal Government is helping to remove those barriers, it also has a responsibility for what happens after they are reduced. We must see to it that our approach to health problems is a balanced approach. We must be sure that our health care system is ready and able to welcome its new clients.

3. *Organizing for Efficiency*. As we move toward these goals, we must recognize that we *cannot* simply *buy* our way to better medicine. We have already been trying that too long. We have been persuaded, too often, that the plan that costs the most will help the most and too often we have been disappointed.

We cannot be accused of having underfinanced our medical system—not by a long shot. We have, however, spent this money poorly—reenforcing inequities and rewarding inefficiencies and placing the burden of greater new demands on the same old system which could not meet the old ones.

The toughest question we face then is not *how much* we should spend but *how* we should spend it. It must be our goal not merely to finance a more expensive medical system but to organize a more efficient one.

There are two particularly useful ways of doing this:

A. *Emphasizing Health Maintenance*. In most cases our present medical system operates episodically—people come to it in moments of distress—when they require its most expensive services. Yet both the system and those it serves would be better off if less expensive services could be delivered on a more regular basis.

If more of our resources were invested in preventing sickness and accidents, fewer would have to be spent on costly cures. If we gave more attention to treating illness in its early stages, then we would be less troubled by acute disease. In short, we should build a true "health" system—and not a "sickness" system alone. We should work to maintain health and not merely to restore it.

B. *Preserving Cost Consciousness*. As we determine just who should bear the various costs of health care, we should remember that only as people are aware of those costs will they be motivated to reduce them. When consumers pay virtually nothing for services and when, at the same time, those who provide services know that all *their* costs will also be met, then neither the consumer nor the provider has an incentive to use the system efficiently. When that happens, unnecessary demand can multiply, scarce resources can be squandered and the shortage of services can become even more acute.

Those who are hurt the most by such developments are often those whose medical needs are most pressing. While costs should never be a barrier to providing needed care, it is important that we preserve some element of cost consciousness within our medical system.

4. *Building on Strengths*. We should also avoid holding the whole of our health care system responsible for failures in some of its parts. There is a natural temptation in dealing with any complex problem to say: "Let us wipe the slate clean and start from scratch." But to do this—to dismantle our entire health insurance system, for example—would be to ignore those important parts of the system which have provided useful service. While it would be wrong to ignore any weaknesses in our present system, it would be equally wrong to sacrifice its strengths.

One of those strengths is the diversity of our system—and the range of choice it therefore provides to doctors and patients alike. I believe the public will always be better served by a pluralistic system than by a monolithic one, by a system which creates many effective centers of responsibility—both public and private—rather than one that concentrates authority in a single governmental source.

This does not mean that we must allow each part of the system to go its own independent way, with no sense of common purpose. We must encourage greater cooperation and build better coordination—but not by fostering uniformity and eliminating choice. One effective way of influencing the system is by structuring *incentives* which reward people for helping to achieve national goals without forcing their decisions or dictating the way they are carried out. The American people have always shown a unique capacity to move toward common goals in varied ways. Our efforts to reform health care in America will be more effective if they build on this strength.

These, then, are certain cardinal principles on which our National Health Strategy should be built. To implement this strategy, I now propose for the consideration of the Congress the following six point program. It begins with measures designed to increase and improve the supply of medical care and concludes with a program which will help people pay for the care they require.

A. Reorganizing the Delivery of Service

In recent years, a new method for delivering health services has achieved growing respect. This new approach has two essential attributes. It brings together a comprehensive range of medical services in a single organization so that a patient is assured of convenient access to all of them. And it provides needed services for a fixed contract fee which is paid in advance by all subscribers.

Such an organization can have a variety of forms and names and sponsors. One of the strengths of this new concept, in fact, is its great flexibility. The general term which has been applied to all of these units is "HMO"—Health Maintenance Organization.

The most important advantage of Health Maintenance Organizations is that they increase the value of the services a consumer receives for each health dollar. This happens, first, because such organizations provide a strong financial incentive for better preventive care and for greater efficiency.

Under traditional systems, doctors and hospitals are paid, in effect, on a piece work basis. The more illnesses they treat—and the more service they render—the more their income rises. This does not mean, of course, that they do any less than their very best to *make* people well. But it does mean that there is no economic incentive for them to concentrate on keeping *people* healthy.

A fixed-price contract for comprehensive care reverses this illogical incentive. Under this arrangement, income grows not with the number of days a person is sick but with the number of days he is well. HMO's therefore have a strong financial interest in preventing illness, or, failing that, in treating it in its early stages, promoting a thorough recovery and preventing any reoccurrence. Like doctors in ancient China, they are paid to keep their clients healthy. For them, economic interests work to reenforce their professional interests.

At the same time, HMO's are motivated to function more efficiently. When providers are paid retroactively for each of their services, inefficiencies can often be subsidized. Sometimes, in fact, inefficiency is rewarded—as when a patient who does not need to be hospitalized is treated in a hospital so that he can collect on his insurance. On the other hand, if an HMO is wasteful of time or talent or facilities, it cannot pass those extra costs on to the consumer or to an insurance company. Its budget for the year is determined in advance by the number of its subscribers. From that point on it is penalized for going over its budget and rewarded for staying under it.

In an HMO, in other words, cost consciousness is fostered. Such an organization cannot afford to waste resources—that costs more money in the short run. But neither can it afford to economize in ways which hurt patients—for that increases long-run expenses.

The HMO also organizes medical resources in a way that is more convenient for patients and more responsive to their needs. There was a time when every housewife had to go to a variety of shops and markets and pushcarts to buy her family's groceries. Then along came the supermarket—making her shopping chores much easier and also giving her a wider range of choice and lower prices. The HMO provides similar advantages in the medical field. Rather than forcing the consumer to thread his way through a complex maze of separate services and specialists, it makes a full range of resources available through a single organization—often at a single stop—and makes it more likely that the right combination of resources will be utilized.

Because a team can often work more efficiently than isolated individuals, each doctor's energies go further in a Health Maintenance Organization—twice as far according to some studies. At the same time, each patient retains the freedom to choose his own personal doctor. In addition, services can more easily be made available at night and on weekends in an HMO. Because many doctors often use the same facilities and equipment and can share the expense of medical assistants and business personnel, overhead costs can be sharply curtailed. Physicians benefit from the stimulation that comes from working with fellow professionals who can share their problems, appreciate their accomplishments and readily offer their counsel and assistance. HMO's offer doctors other advantages as well, including a more regular work schedule, better opportunities for continuing education, lesser financial risks upon first entering practice, and generally lower rates for malpractice insurance.

Some seven million Americans are now enrolled in HMO's—and the number is growing. Studies show that they are receiving high quality care at a significantly lower cost—as much as one-fourth to one-third lower than traditional care in some areas. They go to hospitals less often and they spend less time there when they go. Days spent in the hospital each year for those who belong to HMO's are only three-fourths of the national average.

Patients and practitioners alike are enthusiastic about this organizational concept. So is this Administration. That is why we proposed legislation last March to enable Medicare recipients to join such programs. That is why I am now making the following additional recommendations:

1. We should require public and private health insurance plans to allow beneficiaries to use their plan to purchase membership in a Health Maintenance Organization when one is available. When, for example, a union and an employer negotiate a contract which includes health insurance for all workers, each worker should have the right to apply the actuarial value of his coverage toward the purchase of a fixed-price, health maintenance program. Similarly, both Medicare and the new Family Health Insurance Plan for the poor which I will set out later in this message should provide an HMO option.

2. To help new HMO's get started—an expensive and complicated task— we should establish a new $23 million program of planning grants to aid potential sponsors—in both the private and public sector.

3. At the same time, we should provide additional support to help sponsors raise the necessary capital, construct needed facilities, and sustain initial operating deficits until they achieve an enrollment which allows them to pay their own way. For this purpose, I propose a program of Federal loan guarantees which will enable private sponsors to raise some $300 million in private loans during the first year of the program.

4. Other barriers to the development of HMO's include archaic laws in 22 States which prohibit or limit the group practice of medicine and laws in most States which prevent doctors from delegating certain responsibilities (like giving injections) to their assistants. To help remove such barriers, I am instructing the Secretary of Health, Education and Welfare to develop a model statute which the States themselves can adopt to correct these anomalies. In addition, the Federal Government will facilitate the development of HMO's in all States by entering into contracts with them to provide service to Medicare recipients and other Federal beneficiaries who elect such programs. Under the supremacy clause of the Constitution, these contracts will operate to preempt any inconsistent State statutes.

Our program to promote the use of HMO's is only one of the efforts we will be making to encourage a more efficient organization of our health care system. We will take other steps in this direction, including stronger efforts to capitalize on new technological developments.

In recent years medical scientists, engineers, industrialists, and management experts have developed many new techniques for improving the efficiency and effectiveness of health care. These advances include automated devices for measuring and recording body functions such as blood flow and the electrical activity of the heart, for performing laboratory tests and making the results readily available to the doctor, and for reducing the time required to obtain a patient's medical history. Methods have also been devised for using computers in diagnosing diseases, for monitoring and diagnosing patients from remote locations, for keeping medical records and generally for restructuring the layout and administration of hospitals and other care centers. The results of early tests for such techniques have been most promising. If new developments can be widely implemented, they can help us deliver more effective, more efficient care at lower prices.

The hospital and outpatient clinic of tomorrow may well bear little resemblance to today's facility. We must make every effort to see that its full promise is realized. I am therefore directing the Secretary of Health, Education and Welfare to focus research in the field of health care services on new techniques for improving the productivity of our medical system. The Department will establish pilot experiments and demonstration projects in this area, disseminate the results of this work, and encourage the health industry and the medical profession to bring such techniques into full and effective use in the health care centers of the nation.

B. Meeting the Special Needs of Scarcity Areas

Americans who live in remote rural areas or in urban poverty neighborhoods often have special difficulty obtaining adequate medical care. On the average, there is now one doctor for every 630 persons in America. But in over one-third of our counties the number of doctors per capita is less than one-third that high. In over 130 counties, comprising over eight percent of our land area, there are no private doctors at all—and the number of such counties is growing.

A similar problem exists in our center cities. In some areas of New York for example, there is one private doctor for every 200 persons but in other areas the ratio is one to 12,000. Chicago's inner city neighborhoods have some 1700 fewer physicians today than they had ten years ago.

How can we attract more doctors—and better facilities—into these scarcity areas? I propose the following actions:

1. We should encourage Health Maintenance Organizations to locate in scarcity areas. To this end, I propose a $22 million program of direct Federal grants and loans to help offset the special risks and special costs which such projects would entail.

2. When necessary, the Federal Government should supplement these efforts by supporting out-patient clinics in areas which still are underserved. These units can build on the experience of the Neighborhood Health Centers experiment which has now been operating for several years. These facilities would serve as a base on which full HMO's—operating under other public or private direction—could later be established.

I have also asked the Administrator of Veterans Affairs and the Secretary of Health, Education, and Welfare to develop ways in which the Veterans Administration medical system can be used to supplement local medical resources in scarcity areas.

3. A series of new area Health Education Centers should also be established in places which are medically underserved—as the Carnegie Commission on Higher Education has recommended. These centers would be satellites of existing medical and other health science schools; typically, they could be built around a community hospital, a clinic or an HMO which is already in existence. Each would provide a valuable teaching center for new health

professionals, a focal point for the continuing education of experienced personnel, and a base for providing sophisticated medical services which would not otherwise be available in these areas. I am requesting that up to $40 million be made available for this program in Fiscal Year 1972.

4. We should also find ways of compensating—and even rewarding—doctors and nurses who move to scarcity areas, despite disadvantages such as lower income and poorer facilities.

As one important step in this direction, I am proposing that our expanding loan programs for medical students include a new forgiveness provision for graduates who practice in a scarcity area, especially those who specialize in primary care skills that are in short supply.

In addition, I will request $10 million to implement the Emergency Health Personnel Act. Such funds will enable us to mobilize a new National Health Service Corps, made up largely of dedicated and public-spirited young health professionals who will serve in areas which are now plagued by critical manpower shortages.

Meeting the Personnel Needs of our Growing Medical System

Our proposals for encouraging HMO's and for serving scarcity areas will help us use medical manpower more effectively. But it is also important that we *produce* more health professionals and that we educate more of them to perform critically needed services. I am recommending a number of measures to accomplish these purposes.

1. First, we must use new methods for helping to finance medical education. In the past year, over half of the nation's medical schools have declared that they are in "financial distress" and have applied for special Federal assistance to meet operating deficits.

More money is needed—but it is also important that this money be spent in new ways. Rather than treating the symptoms of distress in a piecemeal and erratic fashion, we must rationalize our system of financial aid for medical education so that the schools can make intelligent plans for regaining a sound financial position.

I am recommending, therefore, that much of our present aid to schools of medicine, dentistry and osteopathy—along with $60 million in new money—be provided in the form of so-called "capitation grants," the size of which would be determined by the number of students the school graduates. I recommend that the capitation grant level be set at $6,000 per graduate.

A capitation grant system would mean that a school would know in advance how much Federal money it could count on. It would allow an institution to make its own long-range plans as to how it would use these monies. It would mean that we could eventually phase out our emergency assistance programs.

By rewarding *output*—rather than subsidizing *input*—this new aid system would encourage schools to educate more students and to educate them more efficiently. Unlike formulas which are geared to the annual number of enrollees, capitation grants would provide a strong incentive for schools to shorten their curriculum from four years to three—in line with another sound recommendation of the Carnegie Commission on Higher Education. For then, the same sized school would qualify for as much as one-third *more* money each year, since each of its graduating classes would be one-third larger.

This capitation grant program should be supplemented by a program of special project grants to help achieve special goals. These grants would support efforts such as improving planning and management, shortening curriculums, expanding enrollments, team training of physicians and allied health personnel, and starting HMO's for local populations.

In addition, I believe that Federal support dollars for the construction of medical education facilities can be used more effectively. I recommend that the five current programs in this area be consolidated into a single, more flexible grant authority and that a new program of guaranteed loans and other financial aids be made available to generate over $500 million in private construction loans in the coming Fiscal Year—five times the level of our current construction grant program.

Altogether, these efforts to encourage and facilitate the expansion of our medical schools should produce a 50 percent increase in medical school graduates by 1975. We must set that as our goal and we must see that it is accomplished.

2. The Federal Government should also establish special support programs to help low income students enter medical and dental schools. I propose that our scholarship grant program for these students be almost doubled—from $15 to $29 million. At the same time, this Administration would modify its proposed student loan programs better to meet the needs of medical students. To help alleviate the concern of low income students that such a loan might become an impossible burden if they fail to graduate from medical school, we will request authority to forgive loans where such action is appropriate.

3. One of the most promising ways to expand the supply of medical care and to reduce its costs is through a greater use of allied health personnel, especially those who work as physicians' and dentists' assistants, nurse pediatric practitioners, and nurse midwives. Such persons are trained to perform tasks which must otherwise be performed by doctors themselves, even though they do not require the skills of a doctor. Such assistance frees a physician to focus his skills where they are most needed and often allows him to treat many additional patients.

I recommend that our allied health personnel training programs be expanded by 50% over 1971 levels, to $29 million, and that $15 million of this amount be devoted to training physicians' assistants. We will also encourage medical schools to train future doctors in the proper use of such assistants and we will take the steps I described earlier to eliminate barriers to their use in the laws of certain States.

In addition, this administration will expand nationwide the current MEDIHC program—an experimental effort to encourage servicemen and women with medical training to enter civilian medical professions when they leave military duty. Of the more than 30,000 such persons who leave military service each year, two-thirds express an interest in staying in the health field but only about one-third finally do so. Our goal is to increase the number who enter civilian health employment by 2,500 per year for the next five years. At the same time, the Veterans Administration will expand the number of health trainees in VA facilities from 49,000 in 1970 to over 53,000 in 1972.

D. A Special Problem: Malpractice Suits and Malpractice Insurance

One reason consumers must pay more for health care and health insurance these days is the fact that most doctors are paying much more for the insurance *they* must buy to protect themselves against claims of malpractice. For the past *five* years, malpractice insurance rates have gone up an average of 10 percent a year—a fact which reflects both the growing number of malpractice claims and the growing size of settlements. Many doctors are having trouble obtaining *any* malpractice insurance.

The climate of fear which is created by the growing menace of malpractice suits also affects the quality of medical treatment. Often it forces doctors to practice inefficient, defensive medicine—ordering unnecessary tests and treatments solely for the sake of appearance. It discourages the use of physicians' assistants, inhibits that free discussion of cases which can contribute so much to better care, and makes it harder to establish a relationship of trust between doctors and patients.

The consequences of the malpractice problem are profound. It must be confronted soon and it must be confronted effectively—but that will be no simple matter. For one thing, we need to know far more than we presently do about this complex problem.

I am therefore directing—as a first step in dealing with this danger—that the Secretary of Health, Education and Welfare promptly appoint and convene a Commission on Medical Malpractice to undertake an intensive program of research and analysis in this area. The Commission memberships should represent the health professions and health institutions, the legal profession, the insurance industry, and the general public. Its report—which should include specific recommendations for dealing with this problem—should be submitted by March 1, 1972.

E. New Actions to Prevent Illnesses and Accidents

We often invest our medical resources as if an ounce of cure were worth a pound of prevention. We spend vast sums to treat illnesses and accidents that could be avoided for a fraction of those expenditures. We focus our attention on *making* people well rather than *keeping* people well, and—as a result—both our health and our pocketbooks are poorer. A new National Health Strategy should assign a much higher priority to the work of prevention.

As we have already seen, Health Maintenance Organizations can do a great deal to help in this effort. In addition to encouraging their growth, I am also recommending a number of further measures through which we can take the offensive against the long-range causes of illnesses and accidents.

1. To begin with, we must reaffirm—and expand—the Federal commitment to biomedical research. Our approach to research support should be balanced—with strong efforts in a variety of fields. Two critical areas, however, deserve special attention.

The first of these is cancer. In the next year alone, 650,000 new cases of cancer will be diagnosed in this country and 340,000 of our people will die of this disease. Incredible as it may seem, one out of every four Americans who are now alive will someday develop cancer unless we can reduce the present rates of incidence.

In the last seven years we spent more than 30 billion dollars on space research and technology and about one-twenty-fifth of that amount to find a cure for cancer. The time has now come to put more of our resources into cancer research and—learning an important lesson from our space program— to organize those resources as effectively as possible.

When we began our space program we were fairly confident that our goals could be reached if only we made a great enough effort. The challenge was technological; it did not require new theoretical breakthroughs. Unfortunately, this is not the case in most biomedical research at the present time; scientific breakthroughs are still required and they often cannot be forced— no matter how much money and energy is expended.

We should not forget this caution. At the same time, we should recognize that of all our research endeavors, cancer research may now be in the best position to benefit from a great infusion of resources. For there are moments in biomedical research when problems begin to break open and results begin to pour in, opening many new lines of inquiry and many new opportunities for breakthrough.

We believe that cancer research has reached such a point. This Administration is therefore requesting an additional $100 million for cancer research in its new budget. And—as I said in my State of the Union Message—"I will ask later for whatever additional funds can effectively be used" in this effort.

Because this project will require the coordination of scientists in many fields—drawing on many projects now in existence but cutting across established organizational lines—I am directing the Secretary of Health, Education and Welfare to establish a new Cancer Conquest Program in the Office of the Director of the National Institutes of Health. This program will operate under its own Director who will be appointed by the Secretary and supported by a new management group. To advise that group in establishing priorities and allocating funds—and to advise other officials, including me, concerning this effort—I will also establish a new Advisory Committee on the Conquest of Cancer.

A second targeted disease for concentrated research should be sickle cell anemia—a most serious childhood disease which almost always occurs in the black population. It is estimated that one out of every 500 black babies actually develops sickle cell disease.

It is a sad and shameful fact that the causes of this disease have been largely neglected throughout our history. We cannot rewrite this record of neglect, but we can reverse it. To this end, this Administration is increasing its budget for research and treatment of sickle cell disease fivefold, to a new total of $6 million.

2. A second major area of emphasis should be that of health education.

In the final analysis, each individual bears the major responsibility for his own health. Unfortunately, too many of us fail to meet that responsibility.

Too many Americans eat too much, drink too much, work too hard, and exercise too little. Too many are careless drivers.

These are personal questions, to be sure, but they are also public questions. For the whole society has a stake in the health of the individual. Ultimately, everyone shares in the cost of his illnesses or accidents. Through tax payments and through insurance premiums, the careful subsidize the careless, the nonsmokers subsidize those who smoke, the physically fit subsidize the rundown and the overweight, the knowledgeable subsidize the ignorant and vulnerable.

It is in the interest of our entire country, therefore, to educate and encourage each of our citizens to develop sensible health practices. Yet we have given remarkably little attention to the health education of our people. Most of our current efforts in this area are fragmented and haphazard—a public service advertisement one week, a newspaper article another, a short lecture now and then from the doctor. There is no national instrument, no central force to stimulate and coordinate a comprehensive health education program.

I have therefore been working to create such an instrument. It will be called the National Health Education Foundation. It will be a private, nonprofit group which will receive no Federal money. Its membership will include representatives of business, labor, the medical profession, the insurance industry, health and welfare organizations, and various governmental units. Leaders from these fields have already agreed to proceed with such an organization and are well on the way toward reaching an initial goal of $1 million in pledges for its budget.

This independent project will be complemented by other Federal efforts to promote health education. For example, expenditures to provide family planning assistance have been increased, rising fourfold since 1969. And I am asking that the great potential of our nation's day care centers to provide health education be better utilized.

3. We should also expand Federal programs to help prevent accidents—the leading cause of death between the ages of one and 37 and the fourth leading cause of death for persons of all ages.

Our highway death toll—50,000 fatalities last year—is a tragedy and an outrage of unspeakable proportions. It is all the more shameful since half these deaths involved drivers or pedestrians under the influence of alcohol. We have therefore increased funding for the Department of Transportation's auto accident and alcohol program from $8 million in Fiscal Year 1971 to $35 million in Fiscal Year 1972. I am also requesting that the budget for alcoholism programs be doubled, from $7 million to $14 million. This will permit an expansion of our research efforts into better ways of treating this disease.

I am also requesting a supplemental appropriation of $5 million this year and an addition of $8 million over amounts already in the 1972 budget to implement aggressively the new Occupational Safety and Health Act I signed last December. We must begin immediately to cut down on the 14,000 deaths and more than two million disabling injuries which result each year from occupational illnesses and accidents.

The conditions which affect health are almost unlimited. A man's income, his daily diet, the place he lives, the quality of his air and water—all of these factors have a greater impact on his physical well-being than does the family doctor. When we talk about our health program, therefore, we should not forget our efforts to protect the nation's food and drug supply, to control narcotics, to restore and renew the environment, to build better housing and transportation systems, to end hunger in America, and—above all—to place a floor under the income of every family with children. In a sense this special message on health is one of *many* health messages which this Administration is sending to the Congress.

F. A National Health Insurance Partnership

In my State of the Union message, I pledged to present a program "to ensure that no American family will be prevented from obtaining basic medical care by inability to pay." I am announcing that program today. It is a comprehensive national health insurance program, one in which the public and the private sectors would join in a new partnership to provide adequate health insurance for the American people.

In the last twenty years, the segment of our population owning health insurance has grown from 50 percent to 87 percent and the portion of medical bills paid for by insurance has gone from 35 percent to 60 percent. But despite this impressive growth, there are still serious gaps in present health insurance coverage. Four such gaps deserve particular attention.

First—too many health insurance policies focus on hospital and surgical costs and leave critical outpatient services uncovered. While some 80 percent of our people have some hospitalization insurance, for example, only about half are covered for outpatient and laboratory services and less than half are insured for treatment in the physician's office or the home. Because demand goes where the dollars are, the result is an unnecessary—and expensive—overutilization of acute care facilities. The average hospital stay today is a full day longer than it was eight years ago. Studies show that over one-fourth of hospital beds in some areas are occupied by patients who do not really need them and could have received equivalent or better care outside the hospital.

A second problem is the failure of most private insurance policies to protect against the catastrophic costs of major illnesses and accidents. Only 40 percent of our people have catastrophic cost insurance of any sort and most of that insurance has upper limits of $10,000 or $15,000. This means that insurance often runs out while expenses are still mounting. For many of our families, the anguish of a serious illness is thus compounded by acute financial anxiety. Even the joy of recovery can often be clouded by the burden of debt—and even by the threat of bankruptcy.

A third problem with much of our insurance at the present time is that it cannot be applied to membership in a Health Maintenance Organization—and thus effectively precludes such membership. No employee will pay to join such a plan, no matter how attractive it might seem to him, when deductions from his paycheck—along with contributions from his employer—are being used to purchase another health insurance policy.

The fourth deficiency we must correct in present insurance coverage is its failure to help the poor gain sufficient access to our medical system. Just one index of this failure is the fact that fifty percent of poor children are not even immunized against common childhood diseases. The disability rate for families below the poverty line is at least 50 percent higher than for families with incomes above $10,000.

Those who need care most often get care least. And even when the poor do get service, it is often second rate. A vicious cycle is thus reinforced—poverty breeds illness and illness breeds greater poverty. This situation will be corrected only when the poor have sufficient purchasing power to enter the medical marketplace on equal terms with those who are more affluent.

Our National Health Insurance Partnership is designed to correct these inadequacies—not by *destroying* our present insurance system but by *improving* it. Rather than giving up on a system which has been developing impressively, we should work to bring about further growth which will fill in the gaps we have identified. To this end, I am recommending the following combination of public and private efforts.

1. I am proposing that a National Health Insurance Standards Act be adopted which will require employers to provide basic health insurance coverage for their employees.

In the past, we have taken similar actions to assure workers a minimum wage, to provide them with disability and retirement benefits, and to set occupational health and safety standards. Now we should go one step further and guarantee that all workers will receive adequate health insurance protection.

The minimum program we would require under this law would pay for hospital services, for physicians' services—both in the hospital and outside of it, for full maternity care, well-baby care (including immunizations), laboratory services and certain other medical expenses. To protect against catastrophic costs, benefits would have to include not less than $50,000 in coverage for each family member during the life of the policy contract. The minimum package would include certain deductible and coinsurance features. As an alternative to paying separate fees for separate services, workers could use this program to purchase membership in a Health Maintenance Organization.

The Federal Government would pay nothing for this program; the costs would be shared by employers and employees, much as they are today under most collective bargaining agreements. A ceiling on how much employees could be asked to contribute would be set at 35 percent during the first two and one-half years of operation and 25 percent thereafter. To give each employer time to plan for this additional cost of doing business—a cost which would be shared, of course, by all of his competitors—this program would not go into effect until July 1, 1973. This schedule would also allow time for expanding and reorganizing our health system to handle the new requirements.

As the number of enrollees rises under this plan, the costs per enrollee can be expected to fall. The fact that employees and unions will have an even higher stake in the system will add additional pressures to keep quality up and costs down. And since the range within which benefits can vary will be somewhat narrower than it has been, competition between insurance companies will be more likely to focus on the overall price at which the contract is offered. This means that insurance companies will themselves have a greater motivation to keep medical costs from soaring.

I am still considering what further legislative steps may be desirable for regulating private health insurance, including the introduction of sufficient disincentive measures to reinforce the objective of creating cost consciousness on the part of consumers and providers. I will make such recommendations to the Congress at a later time.

2. I am also proposing that a new Family Health Insurance Plan be established to meet the special needs of poor families who would not be covered by the proposed National Health Insurance Standards Act headed by unemployed, intermittently employed or self-employed persons.

The Medicaid program was designed to help these people, but—for many reasons—it has not accomplished its goals. Because it is not a truly national program, its benefits vary widely from State to State. Sixteen States now get 80 percent of all Medicaid money and two States, California and New York, get 30 percent of Federal funds though they have only 20 percent of the poverty population. Two States have no Medicaid program at all.

In addition, Medicaid suffers from other defects that now plague our failing welfare system. It largely excludes the working poor—which means that all benefits can suddenly be cut off when family income rises ever so slightly—from just under the eligibility barrier to just over it. Coverage is provided when husbands desert their families, but is often eliminated when they come back home and work. The program thus provides an incentive for poor families to stay on the welfare rolls.

Some of these problems would be corrected by my proposal to require employers to offer adequate insurance coverage to their employees. No longer, for example, would a workingman receive poorer insurance coverage than a welfare client—a condition which exists today in many States. But we also need an additional program for much of the welfare population.

Accordingly, I propose that the part of Medicaid which covers most welfare families be eliminated. The new Family Health Insurance Plan that takes its place would be fully financed and administered by the Federal Government. It would provide health insurance to all poor families with children headed by self-employed or unemployed persons whose income is below a certain level. For a family of four persons, the eligibility ceiling would be $5,000.

For the poorest of eligible families, this program would make no charges and would pay for basic medical costs. As family income increased beyond a certain level ($3,000 in the case of a four-person family) the family itself would begin to assume a greater share of the costs—through a graduated schedule of premium charges, deductibles, and coinsurance payments. This provision would induce some cost consciousness as income rises. But unlike Medicaid—with its abrupt cutoff of benefits when family income reaches a certain point—this arrangement would provide an incentive for families to improve their economic position.

The Family Health Insurance Plan would also go into effect on July 1, 1973. In its first full year of operation, it would cost approximately $1.2 billion in additional Federal funds—assuming that all eligible families participate. Since States would no longer bear any share of this cost, they would be relieved of a considerable burden. In order to encourage States to use part of these savings to supplement Federal benefits, the Federal Government would agree to bear the costs of administering a consolidated Federal-State benefit package. The Federal Government would also contract with local committees —to review local practices and to ensure that adequate care is being provided in exchange for Federal payments. Private insurers, unions and employees would be invited to use these same committees to review the utilization of their benefits if they wished to do so.

This, then, is how the National Health Insurance Partnership would work: The Family Health Insurance Plan would meet the needs of most welfare families—though Medicaid would continue for the aged poor, the blind and the disabled. The National Health Insurance Standards Act would help the working population. Members of the Armed Forces and civilian Federal employees would continue to have their own insurance programs and our older citizens would continue to have Medicare.

Our program would also require the establishment in each State of special insurance pools which would offer insurance at reasonable group rates to people who did not qualify for other programs: the self-employed, for example, and poor risk individuals who often cannot get insurance.

I also urge the Congress to take further steps to improve Medicare. For one thing, beneficiaries should be allowed to use the program to join Health Maintenance Organizations. In addition, we should consolidate the financing of Part A of Medicare—which pays for hospital care—and Part B—which pays for outpatient services, provided the elderly person himself pays a monthly fee to qualify for this protection. I propose that this charge—which is scheduled to rise to $5.60 per month in July of this year—be paid for instead by increasing the Social Security wage base. Removing this admission cost will save our older citizens some $1.3 billion annually and will give them greater access to preventive and ambulatory services.

WHY IS A NATIONAL HEALTH INSURANCE PARTNERSHIP BETTER THAN NATIONALIZED HEALTH INSURANCE?

I believe that our government and our people, business and labor, the insurance industry and the health profession can work together in a *national partnership* to achieve our health objectives. I do *not* believe that the achievement of these objectives requires the *nationalization* of our health insurance industry.

To begin with, there simply is no *need* to eliminate an entire segment of our private economy and at the same time add a multibillion dollar responsibility to the Federal budget. Such a step should not be taken unless all other steps have failed.

More than that, such action would be dangerous. It would deny people the right to choose how they will pay for their health care. It would remove competition from the insurance system—and with it an incentive to experiment and innovate.

Under a nationalized system, only the Federal Government would lose when inefficiency crept in or when prices escalated; neither the consumer himself, nor his employer, nor his union, nor his insurance company would have any further stake in controlling prices. The only way that utilization could be effectively regulated and costs effectively restrained, therefore, would be if the Federal Government made a forceful, tenacious effort to do so. This would mean—as proponents of a nationalized insurance program have admitted—that Federal personnel would inevitably be approving the budgets of local hospitals, setting fee schedules for local doctors, and taking other steps which could easily lead to the complete Federal domination of all of American medicine. That is an enormous risk—and there is no need for us to take it. There is a better way—a more practical, more effective, less expensive, and less dangerous way--to reform and renew our nation's health system.

CONFRONTING A DEEPENING CRISIS

"It is health which is real wealth," said Ghandi, "and not pieces of gold and silver." That statement applies not only to the lives of men but also to the life of nations. And nations, like men, are judged in the end by the things they hold most valuable.

Not only is health more important than economic wealth, it is also its foundation. It has been estimated, for example, that ten percent of our country's economic growth in the past half century has come because a declining death rate has produced an expanded labor force.

Our entire society, then, has a direct stake in the health of every member. In carrying out its responsibilities in this field, a nation serves its own best interests, even as it demonstrates the breadth of its spirit and the depth of its compassion.

Yet we cannot truly carry out these responsibilities unless the ultimate focus of our concern is the personal health of the individual human being. We dare not get so caught up in our systems and our strategies that we lose sight of *his* needs or compromise *his* interests. We can build an effective National Health Strategy only if we remember the central truth that the only way to serve our people well is to better serve each person.

Nineteen months ago I said that America's medical system faced a "massive crisis." Since that statement was made, that crisis has deepened. All of us must now join together in a common effort to meet this crisis—each doing his own part to mobilize more effectively the enormous potential of our health care system.

THE WHITE HOUSE   RICHARD NIXON
February 18, 1971.

APPENDIX C. PROPOSAL FOR PSAC PANEL
ON BIOLOGICAL AND MEDICAL SCIENCE

Federal support for research and education in the biological and medical sciences has slowed in recent years and is now faltering dangerously. There is a growing lack of coordination, approaching confusion, among *national goals* in therapeutic and preventive medicine, delivery of health care, improvement of environmental quality, mental health, nutrition, etc., the quality of the *programs* to achieve them, and the *resources* allocated to this purpose. The disarray among biological scientists and institutions, intramural and extramural, which has been sporadic in recent years, is now generalized. It is urgent that policies and programs in biomedical science be reexamined in depth. A PSAC panel might undertake to do a study around the following questions:

1. What should be the federal policies for support of biological and medical research, professional education in medicine, scientific training in the biological and medical sciences, and delivery of health care to the population?

2. What are the appropriate subjects for biomedical research in the various departments and agencies and how do existing programs overlap or needlessly duplicate each other? Are there neglected areas? Are there nonproductive programs that should be phased out or abandoned?

3. What are the areas of future opportunity in the biological sciences? What mechanisms exist to assure that they will be pursued? What new policies are needed to assure that reallocation of resources will not be detrimental to existing programs of merit?

4. Can present patterns of funding, particularly for categorical research, be improved? How can institutional stability and continuity be better assured?

5. Should there be completely separate funding for medical education and biomedical research? Can these resources be uncoupled? Would such uncoupling encourage reforms in medical education which would be more effective, economical and productive?

6. What should be our policies and programs for training biological and medical scientists?

7. What should be our programs and policies for training paramedical and allied health professionals?

8. What is the future role of such expensive planning programs as regional medical programs and partnership for health? What demonstrable improvements have come from them? Should they continue in their present form?

9. Can we develop a rationale for support of basic research, applied research, and development in the biomedical field that will make possible long-term commitment and phasing to avoid sudden cutbacks and abrupt discontinuities?

NOTES

Chapter 1: Introduction

1. Hunter A. Dupree, *Science in the Federal Government* (Cambridge, Mass.: Harvard University Press, 1957).
2. Lewis E. Auerbach, "Scientists in the New Deal: A Pre-war Episode in the relations between Science and Government in the United States," *Minerva* 3 (1965): 457-82.
3. Ibid., p. 467.
4. Ibid.
5. Don K. Price, "Money and Influence: The Links of Science to Public Policy," *Daedalus* 103 (1974): 108.
6. David Z. Beckler, "The Precarious Life of Science in the White House," *Daedalus* 103 (1974): 115-34.
7. U.S., The White House, *Reorganization Plan No. 2*, 29 March 1962; P. L. 94-282, *National Science and Technology Policy, Organization and Priorities Act of 1976*, 11 May 1976.

Chapter 2: Science Advice for the President: A Perspective

1. Vannevar Bush, *Pieces of the Action* (New York: William Morrow and Co. 1970), p. 50.
2. President F. D. Roosevelt to Dr. Vannevar Bush, 17 November 1944, asking for Bush's recommendation on the subject of the government's role in science, in: Vannevar Bush, *Science, the Endless Frontier* (Washington, D.C.: U.S. Office of Scientific Research and Development, 1945; reprint ed., National Science Foundation, 1960), p. 3.
3. U.S., Congress, House, Subcommittee on Science, Research and Development, of the Committee on Science and Astronautics, *Hearings on National Science Policy*, 7 July 1970, p. 7. Testimony of Don K. Price.
4. Bush, *Pieces of the Action*.
5. Bush, *Science, the Endless Frontier*.
6. John R. Steelman, *Science and Public Policy: A Program for the Nation*, Report to the President, 17 October 1947, vols. 1-5.
7. Ibid.

8. U.S., Congress, House, Military Operations Subcommittee, of the Committee on Government Operations, *The Office of Science and Technology*, Report prepared for the Subcommittee by the Science Policy Research Division of the Legislative Reference Service, Library of Congress, March 1967, p. 207.

9. George B. Kistiakowsky, *A Scientist at the White House* (Cambridge, Mass.: Harvard University Press, 1977).

10. U.S. Congress, Senate, Subcommittee on National Policy Machinery, of the Committee on Government Operations, *Organizing for National Security: Science Organization and the President's Office*, Study prepared for the Committee on Government Operations, 87th Cong., 1st sess., 1961.

11. U.S., The White House, *Reorganization Plan No. 2*, 29 March 1962.

12. David Z. Beckler, "The Precarious Life of Science in the White House," *Daedalus* 103 (1974): 115-34.

13. U.S., The White House, *Reorganization Plan No. 1*, 26 January 1973.

14. National Academy of Sciences, *Science and Technology in Presidential Policy-Making (a Proposal)*, Report of the ad hoc Committee on Science and Technology (Washington, D.C.: National Academy of Sciences, June 1974) (hereafter cited as NAS, *Science and Technology in Presidential Policy-Making*).

15. U.S., Congress, House, Committee on Science and Astronautics, *Hearings on Federal Policy, Plans and Organization for Science and Technology*, Part II, June 20, 25, 26, 27; July 9, 10, 16, 18, 1974; U.S., Congress, House, Committee on Science and Technology, *Hearings on the National Science Policy and Organization Act of 1975*, June 10, 11, 17, 19, 23, 1975 (hereafter cited as House Science and Technology Hearings).

16. P. L. 94-282, *National Science and Technology Policy, Organization and Priorities Act of 1976*, 11 May 1976.

17. Ibid., p. 2.

18. NAS, *Science and Technology in Presidential Policy-Making*, p. 65. Testimony of James R. Killian, Jr.

19. Charles L. Schultze, *The Politics and Economics of Public Spending* (Washington, D.C.: The Brookings Institution, 1968).

20. Joseph A. Califano, Remarks made at the Secretary's National HMO Conference, Washington, D.C., 10 March 1978.

21. Hunter A. Dupree, *Science in the Federal Government* (Cambridge, Mass.: Harvard University Press, 1957).

22. Alan T. Waterman, "National Science Foundation: A Ten-Year Resume," *Science* 131 (1960): 1341-54.

23. Ibid., p. 1342.

24. *Technology and the American Economy*, Report of the National Commission on Technology, Automation and Economic Progress, Washington, D.C., February 1966, p. 75.

25. Ibid., p. 105.

26. U.S., Congress, Senate, *Organizing for National Security*.

27. U.S., Congress, House, Committee on Science and Astronautics, *Creation of the Office of Science and Technology (Reorganization Plan No. 2, 1962)*, staff study prepared for the Committee, 15 May 1962.

28. Ibid.

29. Report of the Panel on Science and Technology to President-Elect Nixon and his Incoming Administration, 1968 (unpublished), p. i.

30. U.S., The White House, *Science and Technology: Tools for Progress*, Report of the President's Task Force on Science Policy, April 1970. Letter of transmittal, p. 2.

31. Ibid., p. 9.

32. U.S., The White House, Office of Science and Technology, Report by the Science and Technology Policy Panel of the President's Science Advisory Committee, September 1971 (unpublished), p. 10.

33. NAS, *Science and Technology in Presidential Policy-Making*, p. 4.

34. House Science and Technology Hearings, p. 194. Testimony of Philip Handler, 11 June 1975.

35. U.S., Congress, *H.R. 9058, National Science and Technology Policy and Organization Act of 1975*, 30 July 1975.

36. U.S., The White House, *Fact Sheet, Advisory Groups on Science and Technology*, 12 November 1975, p. 1.

37. Charles E. Lindblom, "The Science of 'Muddling Through,'" *Public Administration Review* 19 (1959): 79–88; idem, "Decision Making in Taxation and Expenditures in Universities," in: National Bureau of Economic Research, *Public Finances: Needs, Sources, and Utilization* (Princeton, N.J.: Princeton University Press, 1961). Universities–National Bureau Conference Series, No. 12; David Braybooke and Charles E. Lindblom, *A Strategy for Decision* (London: Free Press of Glencoe, Collier-Macmillan, 1963).

38. Lindblom, "The Science of 'Muddling Through.'"

39. U.S., The White House, *Toward Balanced Growth: Quantity with Quality*, Report of the National Goals Research Staff, 4 July 1970.

40. Charles E. Merriam, "The National Resources Planning Board: A Chapter in American Planning Experience," *American Political Science Review* 38 (1944): 1075–88; Herbert Stein, "Better Planning for Less," *Wall Street Journal*, 14 May 1975, p. 12.

41. Robert H. Wiebe, *The Segmented Society. An Introduction to the Meaning of America* (New York: Oxford University Press, 1975).

42. Ibid., p. 126.

43. Ibid., p. 158.

44. Ibid.

45. Theodore Lowi, *The End of Liberalism* (New York: W. W. Norton & Co., 1969).

46. Richard E. Neustadt, *Presidential Power* (New York: John Wiley & Sons, 1962).

47. Richard S. Kirkendall, *Social Scientists and Farm Politics in the Age of Roosevelt* (Columbia, Mo.: University of Missouri Press, 1966).

48. Ibid.; U.S., Department of Agriculture, *Economic Research in the Department of Agriculture*, History Branch, Economic and Statistical Analysis Division, Economic Research Service, 12 July 1972.

Chapter 3: National Health Policy

1. *Medical Care for the American People*. The final report of the Committee on the Costs of Medical Care, 31 October 1932. (Chicago: University of Chicago Press, 1932; reprint ed., New York: Arno Press & The New York Times, 1972).

2. David Mechanic, *Public Expectations and Health Care* (New York: John Wiley & Sons, 1972).

3. *Medical Care for the American People*, p. 13.

4. Martin S. Feldstein, *The Rising Cost of Hospital Care*. Paper prepared for the National Center for Health Services Research and Development, Department of Health, Education and Welfare, Washington, D.C., 18 January 1972.

5. Rashi Fein, *The Doctor Shortage. An Economic Diagnosis* (Washington, D.C.: The Brookings Institution, 1967).

6. Data from various editions of the U.S. Census, as reported in: S. S. Mick, "Understanding the Problems of Human Resources in Health, 1925-1927: Recommendations from the Committee on the Costs of Medical Care and Current Realities." Paper prepared for the Conference on Medical Care for the American People; Unfinished Agenda, Georgetown University, Washington, D.C., 1977 (unpublished).

7. Herman M. Somers, "Health Care Costs," in: The American Assembly, Columbia University, B. Jones, ed., *Health of Americans* (Englewood Cliffs, N.J.: Prentice Hall, 1970).

8. Report of the Pre-Inaugural Task Force on Health, 9 January 1969.

9. *A National Program to Conquer Heart Disease, Cancer and Stroke*, Report to the President's Commission on Heart Disease, Cancer and Stroke, Washington, D.C., December 1964.

10. U.S., Department of Health, Education and Welfare, *Responsibility and Responsiveness (II). A Report on the HEW Potential for the Seventies*, by Elliot L. Richardson, Secretary of Health, Education and Welfare, 18 January 1973.

11. Carnegie Commission on Higher Education, *Higher Education and the Nation's Health. Policies for Medical and Dental Education* (New York: McGraw-Hill, 1970). Education (New York: McGraw-Hill, 1970).

12. Ibid.

13. Abraham Flexner, *Medical Education in the United States and Canada*, A Report to the Carnegie Foundation for the Advancement of Teaching, Bulletin no. 4 (New York, 1910), p. 14, and U.S., Department of Health, Education and Welfare, *The Supply of Health Manpower, 1970 Profiles and Projections to 1990*, Health Resources Administration, December 1974, p. 31.

14. Memorandum from John D. Ehrlichman to Secretary of Health, Education and Welfare, Elliot Richardson, 21 July 1970.

15. Memorandum from Kenneth Cole to members of the Domestic Council, establishing the Health Policy Working Group (later known as the Health Policy Review Group), 18 November 1970.

16. Memorandum from Richard P. Nathan to members of the Domestic Council Health Policy Working Group, 20 November 1970.

17. William H. Forbes, "Longevity and Medical Costs," *New England Journal of Medicine* 227 (1967): 71-78.

18. Ibid., p. 78.

19. U.S., Department of Health, Education and Welfare, *Leading Components of Upturn in Mortality for Man, United States, 1952-1967*, National Center for Health Statistics, Publication No. (HSM) 72-1008, Series 20 (1971), U.S. Superintendent of Documents.

20. Archie L. Cochrane, *Effectiveness and Efficiency, Random Reflections on Health Services* (London: The Nuffield Provincial Hospitals Trust, 1972).

21. Lewis Thomas, *Aspects of Biomedical Science Policy*. Address presented at the Fall Meeting, Institute of Medicine, National Academy of Sciences, Washington, D.C., 9 November 1972. (Washington, D.C.: National Academy of Sciences, 1972).

22. Feldstein, *The Rising Cost of Hospital Care*.

23. Thomas McKeown and C. R. Lowe, *An Introduction to Social Medicine* (Oxford: Blackwell Scientific Publications, 1966); Walsh McDermott, Kurt W. Deuschle, and C. R. Barnett, "Health Care Experiment at Many Farms," *Science 175 (1972):* 23-31; R. Auster, I. Leveson, and D. Arachek, "The Production of Health, an Exploratory Study," *Journal of Human Resources* 4 (1969): 411-36.

24. Ibid.; Edward J. Burger, Jr., "The Nation's Health and Expenditures for Health: Thoughts on National Policy," *Journal of Medical Education* 49 (1974): 927-35; Victor

R. Fuchs, *Who Shall Live: Health, Economics and Social Choice* (New York: Basic Books, 1974); "Doing Better and Feeling Worse: Health in the United States," *Daedalus* 106 (1977): 1-261.

25. Nathan Glazer, "Perspectives on Health Care," *Public Interest* 31 (1973): 111.

26. Marc Lalonde, *A New Perspective on the Health of Canadians* (Ottawa: Information Canada, 1975).

27. U.S., Executive Office of the President, *Annual Report of the Council of Economic Advisers*, U.S. Government Printing Office, 1972.

28. Memorandum from Dr. Jesse Steinfeld to members of the Domestic Council Health Policy Review Group, "Federal Biomedical Research Policy," 4 December 1970, pp. 1-2.

Chapter 4: Health-Related Research and Development

1. Robert Berliner, Oral comments made during the course of the Agency review of the HEW budget before the Office of Management and Budget, November 1972.

2. Vannevar Bush, *Science, the Endless Frontier* (Washington, D.C.: U.S. Office of Scientific Research and Development, 1945: reprint ed., National Science Foundation, 1960), p. 16.

3. U.S., Office of Management and Budget, *Special Analyses: Budget of the United States Government, Fiscal Year 1980*, Executive Office of the President, 1979.

4. U.S., Department of Health, Education and Welfare, *Basic Data Relating to the National Institutes of Health, 1975*, March 1975.

5. Don K. Price, *A Political Hypochondriac Looks at the Future of Medicine*, Paper prepared for the Institute of Medicine, National Academy of Sciences, Washington, D.C., 9 May 1973 (Washington, D.C.: National Academy of Sciences, 1973), p. 20.

6. U.S., Department of Health, Education and Welfare, *The Advancement of Medical Research and Education through the Department of Health, Education and Welfare* (The Bayne-Jones Report), Final Study of the Secretary's Consultants on Medical Research and Education, Office of the Secretary, Washington, D.C., 27 June 1958.

7. Ibid., p. 2.

8. Ibid., p. 30.

9. Ibid., p. 13.

10. Ibid., p. 5.

11. Ibid.

12. Ibid.

13. Ibid.

14. *Biomedical Science and Its Administration. A Study of the National Institutes of Health.* (The Wooldridge Report). Report to the President, February 1965, p. 13 (hereafter cited as *The Wooldridge Report*).

15. Ibid.

16. Bush, *Science, the Endless Frontier.*

17. Ibid.

18. U.S., Congress, Senate, Committee on Labor and Public Welfare, *National Program for the Conquest of Cancer*, Report of the National Panel of Consultants on the Conquest of Cancer, S. Doc. 92-99, 14 April 1971.

19. Gershon Fishbein, "The Siege of NIH," *Washingtonian*, April 1974, pp. 67-139; Daniel S. Greenberg, "HEW-NIH Detente, Plus Other Matters," *New England Journal of Medicine* 290 (1974): 755-56.

20. *The Wooldridge Report*, p. 2.

21. U.S., Department of Health, Education and Welfare, Office of the Secretary, *Report of the Secretary's Advisory Committee on the Management of NIH Research Contracts and Grants* (The Ruina Report), Washington, D.C., March 1966, p. 11 (hereafter cited as *The Ruina Report*).

22. Robert H. Ebert, "Biomedical Research Policy – a Pre-evaluation," *New England Journal of Medicine* 289 (1973): 347-51.

23. Stephen P. Strickland, *Politics, Science and Dread Disease* (Cambridge, Mass.: Harvard University Press, 1972).

24. Harry G. Johnson, "Federal support for basic research: some economic issues," in: *Basic Research and National Goals*, Report to the Committee on Science and Astronautics of the U.S. House of Representatives, by the National Academy of Sciences, March 1965 (Washington, D.C.: National Academy of Sciences, 1965).

25. *The Ruina Report.*

26. Ibid., p. 5.

27. Irvine H. Page, "Financing Research by Disease Categories," *Journal of the American Medical Association* 228 (1974): 995-96.

28. U.S., Congress, Senate, *National Program for the Conquest of Cancer*, p. 3.

29. Donald C. Swain, "The Rise of a Research Empire: NIH 1930 to 1950," *Science* 138 (1962): 1233-37.

30. Bush, *Science, the Endless Frontier.*

31. U.S., Department of Health, Education and Welfare, *Resources for Medical Research. Dollars for Medical Research, Sources and Performers, 1947-1966*, Washington, D.C., January 1967.

32. *The Wooldridge Report.*

33. Carnegie Commission on Higher Education, *Higher Education and the Nation's Health. Policies for Medical and Dental Education* (New York: McGraw-Hill, 1970).

34. Ebert, "Biomedical Research Policy."

35. U.S., HEW, *Resources for Medical Research.*

36. National Science Foundation, Report on the *Seminar of Scientific and Technical Manpower Projections*, National Science Board, Hot Springs, Virginia, 16-18 April 1974 (Washington, D.C.: National Science Foundation, 1974).

37. Ibid.

38. Ebert, "Biomedical Research Policy."

39. Carnegie Commission on Higher Education, *Higher Education and the Nation's Health.*

40. Text of a Proposal for PSAC Panel on Biological and Medical Sciences, President's Science Advisory Committee, Washington, D.C., September 1969 (unpublished).

41. U.S., The White House, Office of Science and Technology, "Scientific and Educational Basis for Improving Health," Draft Report of the Panel on Biological and Medical Science of the President's Science Advisory Committee, July 1970 (unpublished).

42. U.S., The White House, Office of Science and Technology, *Scientific and Educational Basis for Improving Health*, Report of the Panel on Biological and Medical Science of the President's Science Advisory Committee, 1972.

43. U.S., The White House, Office of Science and Technology, Draft Report, Panel on Training for Research in the Biomedical Sciences, President's Science Advisory Committee, Washington, D.C., 3 October 1972 (unpublished).

44. U.S., The White House, Office of Science and Technology, *Improving Health Care through Research and Development*, Report of the Panel on Health Services Research and Development of the President's Science Advisory Committee, 1972.

45. Ibid.

46. Greenberg, "HEW–NIH detente."

47. Charles C. Edwards, *Science, Freedom and Accountability*. Oscar Schwidetzky

Lecture, 48th Congress International Anesthesis Research Society, San Francisco, California, 12 March 1974, pp. 14, 17.

48. Charles S. Vestling, "Science and Public Affairs: an Encouraging Trend," *Federation Proceedings* 33 (1974): 1029.

49. American Biology Council, "Contributions of the Biological Sciences to Human Welfare," *Federation Proceedings* 31 (1972) no. 6, pt. II.

50. P. L. 93-352, *National Cancer Act Amendments of 1974*. Title II, 23 July 1974.

51. U.S., Department of Health, Education and Welfare, *DHEW's Research Planning Principles: A Review*. Institute of Medicine, Division of Health Sciences Policy, NIH Publication No. 79-1955, March 1979

52. Ibid.

Chapter 5: The Environment, Health, and Regulation to Protect Health

1. Edward J. Burger, Jr., *Protecting the Nation's Health. The Problems of Regulation* (Lexington, Mass.: Lexington Books, 1976). (This book includes a case study on 2, 4, 5-T.)

2. Report of the Pre-Inaugural Task Force on Resources and the Environment, 5 December 1968, Summary, p. 1.

3. George B. Kistiakowsky, *A Scientist at the White House* (Cambridge, Mass.: Harvard University Press, 1977).

4. U.S., The White House, *Food Additives*, A Report of the President's Science Advisory Committee, 1960.

5. Ibid.

6. U.S., The White House, *Use of Pesticides*, A Report of the President's Science Advisory Committee, 1963.

7. U.S., The White House, *Restoring the Quality of Our Environment*, Report of the Environmental Pollution Panel, President's Science Advisory Committee, 1965.

8. Burger, *Protecting the Nation's Health*; U.S., The White House, Office of Science and Technology, *Report on 2, 4, 5-T*, A Report of the Panel on Herbicides of the President's Science Advisory Committee, 1971; Thomas Whiteside, "A Reporter at Large," *New Yorker*, 7 February 1970; Thomas Whiteside, "Department of Amplification," *New Yorker*, 5 March 1970.

9. U.S., The White House, Press Office, Announcement on 2, 4, 5-T by Lee A. DuBridge, Science Adviser, 24 October 1969.

10. U.S., Congress, Subcommittee on Energy, National Resources and the Environment, of the Committee on Commerce, *Hearings on the Effects of 2, 4, 5-T on Man and the Environment*, 7 April and 15 April, 1970.

11. Ibid.

12. Report of the Advisory Committee on 2, 4, 5-T to the Administrator of the Environmental Protection Agency, 7 May 1971.

13. "2, 4, 5-T, Decision and Emergency Order Suspending Registration for Certain Uses; Suspension Order: Notice of Intent to Cancel Suspended Uses," *Federal Register* 44, no. 32, 15 March 1979, 15874-97.

14. U.S., The White House, Office of Science and Technology, *Cumulative Regulatory Effects of the Cost of Automobile Transportation*, January 1972.

15. U.S., The White House, Office of Science and Technology, Report of the OST-CED ad hoc Committee on Environmental Health Research, June 1972.

16. Irving Selikoff, ed., "Polychlorinated Biphenyls–Environmental Impact: A Review by the Panel on Hazardous Trace Substances, March 1972," *Environmental Research* 5, no. 3 (September 1972): 249-362.

17. U.S., The White House, Science and Technology Policy Office, *Chemicals and Health*, Report of the Panel on Chemicals and Health of the President's Science Advisory Committee, September 1973.

18. Ibid., p. 11.

19. Ibid., p. 6.

20. Ibid.

21. Institute of Medicine, *Food Safety Policy. Scientific and Societal Considerations*, Part 2, Report of the Committee for a Study on Saccharin and Food Safety Policy, National Academy of Sciences (Washington, D.C.: National Academy of Sciences, March 1979).

22. P. L. 91-604, 84 Stat. 1676, 42 U.S.C., *Clean Air Amendments of 1970*, 18 December 1970.

23. 69 Stat. 322, 84th Cong., 1st sess., ch 360 (1955).

24. U.S., Congress, Senate, *Clean Air Act Amendments and Waste Disposal Act*, S. Rept. to Accompany S. 396, 14 May 1965.

25. Ibid., p. 4.

26. Ibid., p. 7.

27. Memorandum from William S. Gouse, Jr., to Edward E. David, Jr., Director, Office of Science and Technology, Executive Office of the President, 9 October 1970.

28. P. L. 94-469, 90 Stat. 2003, *Toxic Substances Control Act*, 11 October 1976.

29. 15 U.S.C., *Federal Hazardous Substances Act*, 1970.

30. Memorandum from Dr. John Buckley, Office of Science and Technology, recommending new legislation to regulate and inform the Government about industrial-level chemicals, 1970.

31. U.S., Executive Office of the President, Council on Environmental Quality, *Draft*, Toxic Substances Control Act, 7 January 1971.

32. U.S., Congress, House, *Environmental Pollution Effects on Health*, H. Doc. 92-241, 92d Cong., 2d sess., Message from the President of the United States, transmitting the Report of the Department of Health, Education and Welfare, and the Environmental Protection Agency on the Health Effects of Environmental Pollution, Pursuant to Title V of Public Law 91-515, 1 February 1972.

33. *Polychlorinated Biphenyls and the Environment*, Interdepartmental Task Force on PCB's, Washington, D.C., May 1972, National Technical Information Service, No. COM-72-10419; U.S., Executive Office of the President, Council on Environmental Quality, *Environmental Quality*, Annual Report of the Council on Environmental Quality, vols. 1971-1975.

34. *Toxic Substances Control Act*, 1976.

35. U.S., The White House, *Fact Sheet on Reorganization Plans No. 3 and 4*, 9 July 1970.

36. Executive Order 11472, "Establishing the Environmental Quality Council and the Citizen's Advisory Committee on Environmental Quality," *Federal Register* 34, no. 105, 3 June 1969, 8693-95.

37. P. L. 91-190, 83 Stat. S. 52, *National Environmental Policy Act of 1969*, 1 January 1970.

38. U.S., The White House, Press release on the establishment of the Council on Environmental Quality, 1 January 1970.

39. Memorandum from George P. Schultz, Director of the Office of Management and Budget, to William D. Ruckelshaus, Administrator of EPA, 21 May 1971.

40. Domestic Study Memorandum #15 from John Ehrlichman to members of the Domestic Council, 16 June 1971.

41. Maurice H. Stans, "Wait a Minute," Address delivered before the National Petroleum Council, 25th Anniversary Meeting, Department of Interior Auditorium, Washington, D.C., 15 July 1971.

42. Memorandum from Maurice H. Stans, Secretary of Commerce, to the President, 28 June 1971; Memorandum from Maurice H. Stans, Secretary of Commerce, to the President, "Costs of Environmental Compliance," 29 June 1971; Memorandum from Russell E. Train, Chairman of the Council on Environmental Quality, to the President, 30 June 1971; Memorandum from Paul W. McCracken, Chairman of the Council of Economic Advisers, to the President, 20 July 1971.

43. Memorandum from Jon M. Huntsman, Staff Director to the President, to John D. Ehrlichman and John Whitaker, The White House, 3 July 1971.

44. Memorandum from George P. Schultz, Director of the Office of Management and Budget, to Heads of Departments and Agencies, 5 October 1971.

45. Executive Order No. 12044, "Improving Government Regulations," *Federal Register* 43, no. 58, 24 March 1978, 12611.

46. American Bar Association, *Federal Regulation: Roads to Reform*, Report by the Commission on Law and the Economy, American Bar Association (Exposure Draft), Washington, D.C., 5 August 1978 (Washington, D.C.: American Bar Association, 1978).

47. Environmental Defense Fund, "Memorandum to the President and other addressees, re: 'Legal Restriction on Presidential Interference in EPA Rulemaking,'" xeroxed (Washington, D.C.: Environmental Defense Fund, 5 September 1978).

48. Memorandum from H. R. Haldeman to Lee A. DuBridge, 21 February 1970.

49. Letter from Senator Charles McC. Mathias, Jr., to Dr. Lee A. DuBridge, 21 February 1970; Letter from Senator John L. McClellan, Chairman, Committee on Government Operations, to Dr. Edward E. David, Director, Office of Science and Technology, 22 July 1971.

50. Memorandum from Robert Finch to Lee A. DuBridge, 6 April 1970.

51. U.S., Department of Health, Education and Welfare, "The Safety Evaluation of Environmental Chemicals: Needs, Opportunities and Suggested Action," Report prepared for the Secretary's Pesticide Advisory Committee, 22 June 1970 (unpublished).

52. U.S., Department of Health, Education and Welfare, "Memorandum from the Ad Hoc Site Evaluation Team to the Secretary's Pesticide Advisory Committee," 23 June 1970.

53. Memorandum from Robert Finch to Lee A. DuBridge, 5 June 1970.

54. Memorandum from Lee A. DuBridge to George Schultz, Director of the Office of Management and Budget, 24 July 1970.

55. Memorandum from Arnold R. Weber, Associate Director, Office of Management and Budget, to Lee A. DuBridge, 21 August 1970.

56. U.S., Congress, House, H.R. 18515, *Amendment to the Appropriations Act for the Department of Labor and the Department of Health, Education and Welfare*, 13 August 1970.

57. Memorandum from Elliot Richardson to John Ehrlichman, 8 June 1971.

Chapter 6: Population and Family Planning

1. Report of the Pre-Inaugural Task Force on Health, 9 January 1969.

2. Report of the Panel on Science and Technology to President-Elect Nixon and his Incoming Administration, 1968 (unpublished).

3. U.S., Congress, House, *Problems of Population Growth*, H. Doc. 91-139, 91st Cong., 1st sess., Message from the President of the United States, relative to Population Growth, Established Population Growth Commission, 18 July 1969.

4. P. L. 91–572, *Family Planning Services and Population Research Act of 1970*, 3 December 1970.

5. P. L. 91-213, *An Act to Establish a Commission on Population Growth and the American Future*, 16 March 1970.

6. *Population and the American Future*, The Report of the Commission on Population Growth and the American Future, Washington, D.C., 27 March 1972.

7. Memorandum from Russell E. Train to John Ehrlichman, 31 March 1972.

8. Memorandum from John Ehrlichman to Edward David, 16 May 1972.

9. *Population and the American Future*, 1972, p. 110.

10. U.S., Department of Health, Education and Welfare, *DHEW Analysis of the Recommendations of the Commission on Population Growth and the American Future*, together with a covering memorandum from Elliot Richardson to John D. Ehrlichman, 2 October 1972.

11. Letter from John D. Rockefeller III, to Edward E. David, Jr., 11 August 1972; Citizen's Committee on Population and the American Future, Press release announcing the formation of the Citizen's Committee on Population and the American Future, 8 August 1972.

12. Memorandum from Leonard Laster, M.D., Office of Science and Technology, to Kenneth R. Cole, Jr., White House Staff, 5 January 1973.

13. U.S., The White House, Office of Science and Technology, Draft position statement on the recommendation of the Commission on Population Growth and the American Future, dealing with population stabilization, 13 December 1972, by Leonard Laster, M.D.

Chapter 7: Some Additional Issues

1. Memorandum from David Beckler, Office of Science and Technology, to members of the President's Science Advisory Committee concerning the proposed Annual Report on Science and Technology, 19 October 1970, p. 1.

2. U.S., Congress, House, *Authorizing Appropriations for Fiscal Year 1971 for Military Procurement, Research, and Development, and for Anti-ballistic Missile Construction: and Prescribing Reserve Strength*, H. Conference Rept. 91-1473, to accompany H.R. 17123, 26 September 1970.

3. Remarks made by spokesmen for the National Aeronautics and Space Administration during the course of testimony to various committees of the U.S. House of Representatives and the U.S. Senate during the early 1960s.

4. U.S., The White House, *Toward Balanced Growth: Quantity with Quality*, Report of the National Goals Research Staff, 4 July 1970.

5. U.S., The White House, Office of Science and Technology, "Annual Report on Science and Technology," April 1971 (unpublished), p. 2.

6. Ibid., overview chapter, p. 4.

7. Ibid., overview chapter, p. 6.

8. Ibid., overview chapter, p. 2.
chapter, p. 2.

9. Ibid., chapter 21, "The Formulation of Federal Policies for Science and Technology," p. 3.

10. Ibid., chapter 24, "Science Policy in the 70's: A Look into the Future," pp. 1-13.

11. U.S., National Science Foundation, *Science and Technology: Annual Report to the Congress*, Washington, D.C., August 1978.

12. Memorandum from John D. Ehrlichman, Assistant to the President for Domestic Affairs, to a number of Cabinet Secretaries and other Agency heads, on a Domestic Council Study – Evaluation of New Technology Opportunities, The White House, 6 July 1971.

13. Ibid.

14. Memorandum from William M. Magruder, Special Consultant to the President, to the Contributors to the New Technology Opportunities Program, Concerning the Organization and Functions of the NTO Program, The White House, 6 December 1971.

Chapter 8: Summing Up

1. U.S., Congress, House, *Reorganization Plan No. 2 of 1962*, H. Doc. 372, 87th Cong., 2nd Sess., 7 pages.

2. George B. Kistiakowsky, "Presidential Science Advising," *Science* 184 (1974): 38-42; Eugene B. Skolnikoff and Harvey Brooks, "Science Advice in the White House? Continuation of a Debate," *Science* 187 (1975): 35-37.

3. National Academy of Sciences, *Science and Technology in Presidential Policy-Making (a Proposal)*, Report of the ad hoc Committee on Science and Technology (Washington, D.C.: National Academy of Sciences, June 1974).

4. Ibid., p. 17.

5. U.S., Congress, Senate, *National Policy and Priorities for Science and Technology Act of 1975*, 94th Cong., 1st Sess., 15 January 1975.

6. Organization for Economic Cooperation and Development, *Experimental Project on Innovation in the Procedures and Structures of Government, an Outline Analysis of Planning Activities in Government*, Background Paper A, Paris, France, 24 October 1974, p. 6.

7. Government of Canada, *Government Organization Act of 1970, Part IV, Ministries and Ministers of State*, SC 1970-71-72, c. 42, Part IV, pp. 851-54.

8. Canada, Parliament, Senate, *A Science Policy for Canada*, Report of the Senate Special Committee on Science Policy (Ottawa: Queen's Printer): Information Canada, vol. 1 (1970); vol. 2 (1972); vol. 3 (1973).

9. Peter Aucoin and Richard French, *Knowledge, Power and Public Policy*, Science Council of Canada Background Study No. 31 (Ottawa: Science Council of Canada, November 1974).

10. Nicholas E. Golovin, "The 'Evaluative Function' in Government," 25 October 1968 (unpublished).

11. Ibid., p. 23.

12. Ibid., p. 24.

13. Ibid.

14. National Academy of Sciences, *Institutions for Effective Management of the Environment*, Report of the Environmental Study Group of the Environmental Studies Board (Washington, D.C.: National Academy of Sciences, 1970).

15. "The Institute for Congress, a Five-Year Experiment," A Proposal for the establishment of a private organization dedicated to systematic analyses of public issues and programs for the Congress, 1973 (unpublished).

16. Golovin, "The 'Evaluative Function' in Government," p. 32.

17. David Z. Beckler, "The Precarious Life of Science in the White House," *Daedalus* 103 (1974): 116.

18. Alan Mencher, "Recent Developments in British Science Policy," in: U.S., Congress, House, Committee on Science and Astronautics, *Hearings on Federal Policy, Plans and Organization for Science and Technology*, Part II (Washington, D.C.: U.S. Government Printing Office, 1974), pp. 815-16.

19. Skolnikoff and Brooks, "Science Advice in the White House?" p. 511.

20. Alan Pifer, "Foundations and Public Policy Formation," President's statement, in: *Annual Report: Carnegie Corporation of New York, 1974* (New York: Carnegie Corporation, 1974).

21. *A Time to Choose: America's Energy Future*, Report of the Energy Policy Project of the Ford Foundation (Cambridge, Mass.: Ballinger Publishing Co., 1974); *Nuclear Power: Issues and Choices*, Report of the Nuclear Energy Policy Study Group, Sponsored by the Ford Foundation (Cambridge, Mass.: Ballinger Publishing Co., 1977); *Energy: The Next Twenty Years*, Report by a Study Group Sponsored by the Ford Foundation (Cambridge, Mass.: Ballinger Publishing Co., 1979); *Energy in America's Future: The Choices Before Us*, Report of the Energy Strategies Project, Resources for the Future, Washington, D.C. (Baltimore: Johns Hopkins University Press, 1979).

INDEX

Abortion, 103

Agency for International Development, population and family planning activities of, 98, 100–101

Agricultural Adjustment Act, 21–22

Agricultural Extension Service, 1

Agriculture, 1, 114

Agriculture, Department of, 1, 74; Bureau of Agricultural Economics of, 21–24; Cotton Conversion Program of, 22–23; early attempts by, at planning for policy making, 21–24; Economic Research Service of, 23–24; environmental issues of, 76, 88–89; involvement of, in issue of 2, 4, 5-T, 78, 79, 81; role of, in regulation, 73; Secretary of, 21, 33; use of former biological warfare facilities by, 95

Air pollution, 73, 86. *See also* Clean Air Act

American Medical Association, 42

Aminotriazole, contamination of cranberries by, 8n, 75–76

Annual Report on Science and Technology, 105–11; background of, 105–8; development of, 107–10; final destiny of, 110–11; important themes of, discussed, 109–10; important trends to be discerned in, 107–8; political perspective of, 105–8; statutory obligation of, in 1976, 111

Antibiotics in animal feeds, 81

Arizona, 78

Army, U.S., 95

Ash, Roy, 89n

Ash Council. *See* Presidential Commission on Executive Reorganization

Aspirin, 79

Atomic Energy Commission, 7, 9, 73–74, 89

Australia, 118

Automobile: and air pollution, 86–87; emissions standards for, 83, 87–88; safety features of, 83

Bayne-Jones report, 51–52

Beckler, David Z., 3–4, 122

Bennett, Ivan, 66

Biomedical research, 39, 45–72; history of federal investments in, 49–52, 54

Biomedical Science and Its Administration, 51–52, 59, 63, 65

Bionetics Corporation, experiments of, on pesticides, 77–79

Birth defects, 77–79, 80n, 81–82

Blue Cross Association, 26

Board of Science Advisers, 3

Budget, federal, 11–13, 40, 45–48

Bundy, McGeorge, Special Assistant for National Security, 9

Bureau of the Budget, 12. *See also* Office of Management and Budget

Burns, Arthur, 99

Bush, Vannevar, 6–7, 49, 53, 62. See also *Science, the Endless Frontier*

Califano, Joseph, 72

Canada, 38–39, 40n, 118, 122–23; Minister of National Health and Welfare, 38;

The Johns Hopkins University Press
This book was composed in IBM Press Roman Medium
text type by Horne Associates from a design by
Susan Bishop. It was printed and bound by Thomson-
Shore, Inc.

Lightning Source UK Ltd.
Milton Keynes UK
UKHW041433150120
357004UK00001B/106/P